SECOND EDITION

Keys
to
the
Classroom

A Teacher's Guide
to the First Month of School

SECOND EDITION

Keys
to
the
Classroom

Carrol Moran
Judy Stobbe
Wendy Baron
Janette Miller
Ellen Moir

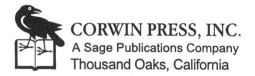
CORWIN PRESS, INC.
A Sage Publications Company
Thousand Oaks, California

For information:

Corwin Press, Inc.
A Sage Publications Company
2455 Teller Road
Thousand Oaks, California 91320
E-mail: order@corwinpress.com

Sage Publications Ltd.
6 Bonhill Street
London EC2A 4PU
United Kingdom

Sage Publications India Pvt. Ltd.
M-32 Market
Greater Kailash I
New Delhi 110 048 India

Printed in the United States of America

Library of Congress Cataloging-in-Publication Data

Keys to the classroom: A teacher's guide to the first month of school /
    by Carrol Moran . . . [et al.].— 2nd ed.
        p. cm.
    English and Spanish.
    ISBN 0-7619-7554-3 (cloth: alk. paper)
    ISBN 0-7619-7555-1 (pbk.: alk. paper)
  1. Elementary school teaching—Handbooks, manuals, etc.
  2. Education, Elementary—Curricula—Handbooks, manuals, etc.
  3. First year teachers—Handbooks, manuals, etc. I. Moran, Carrol.
    LB1555 .K49 2000
    372.1102—dc21   00-008378

This book is printed on acid-free paper.

06   07   08   09   10   9   8   7   6

Corwin Editorial Assistant: Kylee Liegl
Production Editor: Denise Santoyo
Editorial Assistant: Victoria Cheng
Typesetter/Designer: Marion Warren

Contents

Acknowledgments

We would like to thank the many new teachers we worked with in the Santa Cruz County New Teacher Project over the past 10 years for providing the impetus to revise this guide. They freely shared the challenges and frustrations that most teachers face on entering the profession. They showed us very clearly how crucial the first month is in setting the standards of interaction for the rest of the year.

We would also like to thank the following contributors, reviewers, and critics for all of their valuable input: Ellen Wood for her wonderful editing of the revised keys, Marina Cook, Susana Dutro, Pola Espinoza, Liz Gordon, Kathy Idoine, Teri Marchese, Alison Woolpert, and Marney Cox.

In addition, we would also like to thank our typists, Shirlene Campbell, Millie Ashley, and Alice Misumi; our translator, Luz María S. Steves; and our graphic artist, Carrie Wilker, for the wonderful work they have done.

It is our hope in creating this guide that we can ease new teachers' entry into classroom teaching. We want to take the mystery out of the first month, and we have tried to spell out clearly the many keys used by experienced teachers to open the school year successfully.

CARROL MORAN
JUDY STOBBE
WENDY BARON
JANETTE MILLER
ELLEN MOIR

About the Authors

Wendy Baron has taught grades K-6, served as a Title I Reading Specialist, supervised and instructed prospective teachers at the University of California, Santa Cruz, and, for the past 12 years, has worked directly with new teachers through the Santa Cruz New Teacher Project. As Assistant Director of the project, she advises new teachers on a weekly basis, coordinates professional development for 450 beginning teachers, and coaches their advisors. She is one of the coauthors of the statewide training manual, *A Guide to Preparing Support Providers for Work with Beginning Teachers,* and has modeled work with novice teachers in four video documentaries: *Passage into Teaching, Pre-Intern Coach Training, Partnerships in Education,* and *The California Formative Assessment and Support System for Teachers (CFASST).* As Associate Director of the New Teacher Center at the University of California, Santa Cruz, she consults with school districts throughout California on coaching, teacher induction, and designing professional development for beginning teachers.

Janette Miller has extensive training in classroom management, peer coaching, and evaluation. She is a fellow of the Central California Writers' Project and the Monterey Bay Area Math Project. She has particularly enjoyed training novice and veteran teachers in classroom management techniques, direct teaching model, the reading/writing connection, and experiential math strategies. She has been a classroom teacher, a reading specialist, an advisor for the California New Teacher Project, and peer evaluator for new employees in the Santa Cruz City Schools District. She is currently teaching third grade at Westlake School in Santa Cruz.

Ellen Moir is Director of the New Teacher Center at the University of California, Santa Cruz, which is committed to the development of an inspired, dedicated, and highly qualified teaching force by supporting new teachers as they enter the profession. She has served for many years as Director of Teacher Education at UCSC, and since 1988 has directed the Santa Cruz New Teacher Project, which has assisted more than 2,000 beginning teachers to successfully enter California's classrooms. She has produced a number of video documentaries on teacher induction and bilingual education, and has authored numerous articles on teacher development, including beginning teacher support and assessment. She regularly serves as consultant and inspiration keynote speaker to school districts and educational organizations throughout the country, and is a passionate advocate for teacher quality and equitable learning opportunities for all students.

Carrol Moran has worked in education for over 25 years. Her teaching experience encompasses preschool to graduate school, focusing on low-income students of diverse language backgrounds. She earned her BA from Porter College at University of California, Santa Cruz; her Master's Degree in Bilingual Education from San Jose State University; and her PhD in Education, Language Literacy, and Culture, from Stanford University. She has published over 20 articles and books on education, including "Bilingual Education: Broadening Research Perspectives," published in *The Handbook of Research on Multicultural Education* and *A Balanced Approach to Literacy*, a resource document and introduction to K-3 Literacy in teacher-education faculty programs. For the past four years, she has served as Coordinator of the Monterey Bay Educational Consortium, and currently is Director of UCSC's Educational Partnership Center.

Judy Stobbe is currently a classroom teacher and Staff Development Specialist in a Two-Way Bilingual Immersion Program specializing in emergent literacy, effective math instruction, second language acquisition, and effective bilingual education. She has initiated a staff development model based on ongoing teacher collaboration that links authentic assessment to innovative classroom practices across an entire school. In her work as Staff Development Specialist, she has worked with a wide range of teachers—from preservice to those with the most experience. Outside the classroom, she has written curriculum and articles for a variety of publications, including *Into English!: Kindergarten Teacher's Guide, The Bilingual Classroom*, for the DLM Early Childhood Program, *Access to Science: Activities and Strategies for Students Acquiring English Kindergarten-Grade 2*, and, coauthored with Carrol Moran, "Strategies for Working with Overage Students," published in *The Power of Two Languages: Literacy and Biliteracy for Spanish-Speaking Students*. She also serves as an educational consultant across the nation.

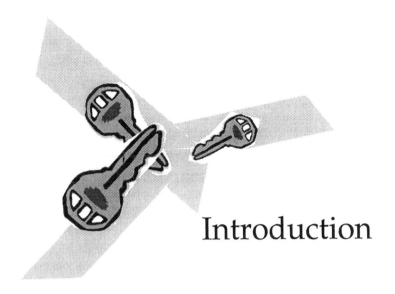

Introduction

Welcome to teaching! The future of our children is now in your hands. You are entering a complex and challenging profession. We believe you deserve as much help as possible to do an outstanding job. *Keys to the Classroom, 2nd Edition* will provide you, the new teacher, essential keys for a successful first year. This second edition of *Keys to the Classroom* incorporates the input of many new and veteran teachers, including a new Chapter 1, "A Guide to Planning," updated assessment materials, new English as a second language materials, and several new classroom activities. We have also added extensive new materials that will assist in planning your first 2 weeks of school and offers a wide assortment of activities from which to choose.

- ☑ Our revised textbook guides you in using your first month as a foundation for a successful year. Following are the elements used to create a rich learning environment:
- ☑ Build a sense of community to include all students
- ☑ Establish clear routines and procedures for your class
- ☑ Assess your students' strengths and needs
- ☑ Create an environment that fosters a love of learning

These elements are at the heart of a good beginning and are important to keep in mind, not only at the start of the school year but throughout it. *Keys to the Classroom's* second edition offers greater detail and a more expanded format than the original text. Following are chapter highlights:

- ☑ Chapter 1, "A Guide to Planning," offers an approach to long-term planning used in establishing the appropriate standards-based context for daily activities. Templates are included to help you think through approaches to each subject area.

☑ Chapter 2, "Creating the Environment," assists you in organizing your classroom and in providing your students with a stimulating learning environment. Also included are suggestions on classroom arrangement and instructional materials.

☑ Chapter 3, "Daily Routines and Procedures," suggests ways to establish both rhythm and structure to your days. Students feel more comfortable when they know what is expected. Clear, consistent routines and procedures eliminate most behavior problems. New teachers often need the most help with this topic. By following the suggested practices, your classroom will run more smoothly.

☑ Chapter 4, "The First Two Weeks of School . . . A Detailed Account " guides you through the first weeks, day by day and minute by minute. This detailed account provides a daily structure, plus a timeline for introducing new routines, procedures and activities. Greater detail to K-1 is provided here, with the assumption that those procedures will be incorporated into other grades. However, as a new teacher, you may wish to read the entire chapter before focusing on yor specific grade level. This chapter is a treasure trove of thoughtful teaching, based on years of teacher experience.

☑ Chapter 5, "Activities for the First Month," describes tried-and-true activities which can be used as the core of your program, or as a back-up plan. Student worksheets, copy-ready, are provided in English and Spanish. These can be included with planned activities or used as "easy assignment" for a substitute.

☑ Chapter 6, "Fingerplays and Songs for Oral Language in English and Spanish," provides community building activities for language development and transitions for K-3 students.

☑ Chapter 7, "Assessments," assists in designing classroom-based assessments. Knowing your students' skills and abilities is crucial in providing them with appropriate instruction.

☑ Chapter 8, "Parent Communications," suggests ways to develop relationships with your parent community and provides a simple letter for adapting to English and Spanish.

☑ Chapter 9, "Resources," offers many excellent books for the advancement of professional development.

Keys to the Classroom is certain to get you off to a good start. In addition to the suggestions and resources provided, we urge you to find an experienced teacher to serve as your mentor—either someone at your grade level, or one with an out-of-classroom position. Their support will be invaluable. New teachers should not attempt this complex job alone. *Find a mentor!*

PHASES OF TEACHING: THE UPS AND DOWNS OF A FIRST-YEAR TEACHER

Over the past decade, the Santa Cruz New Teacher Project (SCNTP) worked with and conducted research on over 2,000 new teachers. Their results will help you understand you are not alone, and that most new teachers have similar struggles during their first year. The project's research shows that new teachers experience five basic phases: (a) anticipation, (b) survival, (c) disillusionment, (d) rejuvenation, and (e) reflection. These are described below, including *new teacher quotes* for each phase. Descriptions are followed with suggestions for moving forward during each particular phase.

Anticipation

This phase begins during the student teaching portion of teacher preparation. New teachers enter with a tremendous commitment to make a difference, coupled with an idealistic view of how their goals will be accomplished: *I was elated to get the job, but terrified about going from the simulated experience of student teaching to that of the person in charge.* (This feeling of excitement often carries new teachers through the first few weeks of school).

Suggestions: Check out as many classrooms as possible. Try to get organized in advance. Set up your classroom environment as soon as you obtain a copy of Keys to the Classroom.

Before starting your teaching assignment, visit a variety of classrooms. If already teaching, search out opportunities to visit other classrooms during recess or lunch for a *reality check.* Your visits will be more meaningful if you have specific questions in mind.

Survival

Your first month may be overwhelming. As a new teacher, you are constantly learning at a rapid pace. New teachers are instantly bombarded with many unanticipated problems and situations. *So little time, so much to learn: I feel like I'm constantly running. It's hard to focus on other aspects of my life.* (It is not uncommon for new teachers to spend up to 70 hrs. per week on schoolwork—with minimal time to reflect on the experience. Particularly overwhelming is the constant need to develop curriculum.)

Suggestions: Time to cut back, save your creative energy for the essentials. Seek out support for time management and organizational strategies.

When in the survival phase, decide where planning can be reduced. Can you borrow an established reading/math curriculum to avoid daily inventing? Or, is it possible to reduce the number of student groups? Reassess your plan now, admitting you are only human and cannot be creative about each curriculum aspect during this first year. Set time limits for planning. Take at least one day off each weekend. Borrow lessons from colleagues, when appropriate, and rely on pre-packaged curriculum.

Disillusionment

New teachers enter this phase following 6-8 weeks of nonstop work and stress of varied length and intensity. Low morale, extensive time commitment, the realization that things are not proceeding as smoothly as they wish—all these contribute to the disenchantment period. At this stage, new teachers begin questioning both their commitment and competence; many become ill. Also during this time, new teachers are confronted with parent conferences, back-to-school night, and their first formal evaluation.

Classroom management may also become a major source of distress: *I thought I'd be focusing more on curriculum, less on classroom management and discipline. I'm stressed because I have some very problematic students who are low academically, and I think about them every second that my eyes are open.*

In this phase, new teachers express self-doubt, have lower self-esteem, face complaints from family and friends, and question their professional commitment. Managing this phase may be the toughest challenge they face as a new teacher.

Suggestions: Double-check your routines and procedures, pare down intricate planning, do something nice for yourself. Remember to breathe! Take care of yourself or you will become ill. Take time to sit on a rock, go for a walk, and listen to music. Working more does not mean life will be smoother. Reduce your level of complexity without decreasing your expectations for students.

This week, a basic math lesson from the book will be fine. Research keys for new activities to carry you through the next few days. *Hints:* get help from a mentor, borrow a lesson plan from another teacher, talk with fellow new teachers—they are experiencing the same thing. You are not alone. You will get through this!

Rejuvenation

This phase is characterized by a rise in new teachers' attitude toward teaching—a fresh sense of hopefulness starting, usually, in January, or following your first extended break. Breaks offer opportunities to relax, reflect, organize materials, and plan curriculum. Teachers acquire a new perspective, with a better understanding of the system, a more realistic acceptance of their teaching, coupled with a sense of accomplishment at having made it through the first, and most difficult, time of the school year. Although still months away, school year's ending becomes the proverbial light at the end of the tunnel. Now, teachers begin to feel more confident about their management skills: *I'm really excited about my story writing center, although my organization has at times been haphazard. Story writing has definitely revived my journals.*

This phase may last into spring, with many ups and downs along the way. Near the end of this time, new teachers worry if all can be accomplished prior to the end of school. Once more questioning their effectiveness as teachers, they wonder how their students will perform on tests: *I'm fearful of these big tests. Can I be fired if my kids do poorly? I don't know enough about them to be cognizant of what I haven't taught, and I'm sure it's a lot.*

Suggestions: Review long-term planning and year-end expectations. This is a good time to take another look at these plans, using more realistic expectations. Also a good time to determine what is expected for year-end exams, so students can be prepared in advance. Discuss your school's expectations for end-of-the-year closing with a mentor, resource teacher, or principal. This helps to spread out wrap-up activities over several months, without being caught off guard during the last month.

Reflection

This phase occurs during the last six weeks of school and can be an invigorating time for first-year teachers. Reflecting back, they can highlight successful events, and review changes to be made the following year in management, curriculum, and teaching strategies. The end is in sight. You've almost made it! More importantly, a vision for your second year emerges—a new phase of anticipation: *Next year, I'd like to start letter puppets earlier, so the kids can be introduced to more letters.*

Suggestions: Take notes on your reflections.

Review what worked and what didn't. Make notes in your plan book to assist in planning the following year. You might think you will never forget this experience, but by the end of summer vacation, all will be a blur. Save yourself from repeating the same mistakes; benefit from new insights to create better lessons. Write it down!

We hope our research helps you realize that your experiences during this first year are normal phases of entering a complex, intense profession—one that cannot be mastered during any first year. Give yourself a break. Rely on *Keys to the Classroom* to get you started. When mistakes occur, remember: Be as kind to yourself as with any student in your classroom. Just like your students, you are doing the best you can!

Have a good first year!

TABLE 1.1

Year at a Glance Matrix

	July	August	September	October	November	December	January	February	March	April	May	June
Theme												
Literacy (Reading)												
Literacy (Writing)												
Math												
Social Studies												
Science												
PE/Health												
Music												
Art												
Assessments												

☑ *Who are my students, and what do they bring?* Surveying students' interests and backgrounds and assessing their skills regularly will enable you to match your instruction to your students. Use your knowledge of their experiences, families, and community to create relevant lessons. Phone each family or visit them at home. Familiarize yourself with the school community.

☑ *What do I want them to know and become able to accomplish?* Knowing your subject matter and having short- and long-term learning goals will help you clarify what to focus your instruction on. Consider which assessments enable you to learn what your students know and are able to accomplish. These should guide the planning, selection, and sequencing of activities and assist in making adjustments to your students' individual needs.

☑ *How will I move them forward?* You will be most successful if you choose a variety of instructional strategies to match what students will learn. Promote critical thinking and problem solving within each lesson. Use resources and materials that *all* students can use and understand, and incorporate learning materials to reflect the linguistic and academic diversity of your classroom. Provide experiences that promote interaction, autonomy, and choice. Teach procedures for each activity within the lesson. Model expected behaviors and provide examples of the quality of work expected of the students.

☑ *How will I know what they have learned?* Use multiple measures for assessing student learning. For example, it is possible to assess students' understanding of concepts through story retellings, written reports, projects, oral presentations, timed tests, work sheets, anecdotal records, written stories, visual displays, and physical demonstrations of skills. Involve students in developing criteria (or a grading system) for completed products by assessing and reflecting on their work and by setting personal learning goals based on their assessments. Use assessment results to guide instruction and to improve your assignments. Involve parents as "assessment partners." Communicate often about their child's progress.

See Tables 1.2 through 1.5 for specific examples of planning tools and activities. To recap the elements basic to midrange planning,

☑ Know the content and subject matter. Determine what students know and are interested in learning.
☑ Use standards to develop goals for student learning.
☑ List possible activities and assessment strategies to develop lessons.

DAILY AND WEEKLY PLANNING

Obtain a copy of both the school and district master schedules ASAP! Enter important dates in your plan book (i.e., Back-to-School Night, report cards, parent conferences, standardized testing dates, staff development days, special holidays, and school and district

(text continued on page 14)

TABLE 1.2

Theme: Getting to Know You; Goals for First Two Weeks

Here are five important goal areas for the first 2 weeks of school. Use this page for brainstorming possible activities and assessments to reach these goals.

Build a Community of Learners	Implement Classroom Procedures and Routines, Including Transition Activities	Establish Standards for Behavior: Rules and Consequences	Teach Reading, Writing, and Math Through a "Getting to Know You" Theme	Assess Students' Knowledge, Skills, Attitudes, and Interests

TABLE 1.3
Theme: Getting to Know You; Possible Activities and Assessments—Intermediate

Build a Community of Learners	Implement Classroom Procedures and Routines	Include Transition Activities	Establish Standards for Behavior: Rules and Consequences	Assessments
Paired Interviews	**Procedures Needed**		**Rules**	**Reading**
Name Games	Getting quiet		Please-Please Don't	Oral Reading and Comprehension Assessment
Find Someone Who . . .	Entering and leaving classroom		Develop four class rules from Please-Please Don't	What I Think About Reading
Graffiti Boards	Equipment checkout		**Literacy**	
Me Pictures	Jobs and monitors		Read aloud vignettes from House on Mango Street	Illustrate rules—individual books	**Writing**
Shields	Snack time and lunch		Morning Messages	Group skits to show examples of rules	Wiggly Line
Partner Drawings	Independent work		Names: scramble, origins, sort		Personal Stories
Name Scramble II	Group work		Think-Alouds—Personal Stories	**Consequences**	What I Think About Writing
	Outside, PE behavior		Personal Stories—Writing Process	*Positive:*	
	Homework			Group points for being at task, being ready	**Math**
	"Transition activities"		**Math**	*Negative:*	Computation
			Graphing Unit (bar, picture, line)	1. Give warning	Problem Solving
	Transition Activities		Letters in name	2. Time out in class	What I Think About Math
	(following recesses):		Month of birthday	3. Recess, other class	
	Sustained Silent Reading		Eye color	4. Call home, meet with parents	**Other**
	Journals		Favorite ice cream (out of three flavors)		Attitude Line-Up, Introducing
	Sentence Corrections		Favorite TV show	**Other**	How I Feel
	Read-Aloud Time		Travel to school	Appreciation Words	
	Math Warm-Ups		Like to be when grown up	Positive Adjectives	
				Conflict Resolution	
				Problem-Solving Skits	

TABLE 1.4

Theme: Getting to Know You; First Week of School—Grades 4 to 6

	Monday	Tuesday	Wednesday	Thursday	Friday
8:30-10:00	Welcome Attention signal Introductions Name Scramble 2 Letters Getting ready for recess	Opening Sentence corrections Literacy—Names	Opening Journals Literacy—House on Mango Street Prewrite "Memorable Moment" Early finishers: SSR, journal, worksheet	Opening Sentence corrections Literacy—Laughter Oral paragraphs First drafts	Opening Journals Literacy—Rice Sandwich Finish first drafts
10:00-10:15	Recess	Recess—Yard Duty	Recess	Recess—Yard Duty	Recess
10:15-11:30	Math Warm-Up Math—Graphing KWL Please-Please Don't Before lunch procedures	Math Warm-Up Math—Bar Graph, "Careers" Please-Please Don't, Part 2	Math Warm-Up Math—students create bar graphs Names Games, Initial Adjectives	SSR Math Warm-Up Math—Line Graph Partner Surveys	Math Warm-Up Math—Circle Graph "What I Think About Math" Survey
11:30-12:15	Lunch	Lunch	Lunch	Lunch	Lunch
12:15-1:30	Read Aloud Know Your Classmates	Read Aloud Partner Drawings	Read Aloud Shields	Read Aloud Finish Shields	Read Aloud What Makes a Good Listener?
1:30-2:30	Homework Jobs PE (knots) Closure and Dismissal	Homework Jobs PE (cooperative relays) Closure and Dismissal	Homework Jobs PE (running laps) Closure and Dismissal	Homework Jobs PE (stretching) Closure and Dismissal	Homework Jobs PE Closure and Dismissal

TABLE 1.5

Theme: Getting to Know You; Second Week of School—Grades 4 to 6

	Monday	Tuesday	Wednesday	Thursday	Friday
8:30–10:00	Opening Sentence corrections Literacy—And Some More Feedback on stories	Opening Journals Literacy—First Job	Opening Sentence corrections Literacy—Core literature	Opening Journals Literacy—Core literature	Opening Sentence corrections Literacy—Core literature "What I Think About Writing"
10:00–10:15	Recess	Recess—Yard Duty	Recess	Recess—Yard Duty	Recess
10:15–11:30	SSR Math Warm-Up Math—begin project What I Think About Reading—survey	SSR Writer's Workshop—peer edit Math Warm-Up Math—develop rubric	SSR Writer's Workshop—final draft Math Warm-Up Math—finish graphs	SSR Writer's Workshop—illustrations Math Warm-Up Math—self-assess and trade graphs	SSR Writer's Workshop—cover, title page, About the Author Math Warm-Up Math—KWL, pretest
11:30–12:15	Lunch	Lunch	Lunch	Lunch	Lunch
12:15–1:30	Read Aloud I Messages	Read Aloud Appreciation Words Graffiti Boards	Read Aloud Problem-Solving Skits	Read Aloud Emotions	Read Aloud Group Definition of Cooperation and Cooperative Triangles
1:30–2:30	Homework PE Jobs Closure and Dismissal	Homework—Line Graphs PE Jobs Closure and Dismissal	Homework PE Jobs Closure and Dismissal	Homework PE Jobs Closure and Dismissal	Homework PE Jobs Closure and Dismissal

events). Learn your school's bell schedule, library time, restructured days, and mandated time for specific subjects. Plan carefully so your daily schedule will remain constant throughout the year (see Table 1.6 for an example).

Daily Calendar

Create a daily calendar showing your bell schedule for recesses and lunch. Include all known times: library, PE, music, and so forth.

Subject Schedule

Determine the schedule for individual subjects, combination of subjects, or themes (a sample primary morning schedule is given in Table 1.6). Consider a possible theme time integrating social studies, language arts, music, and art during the day. Determine how your schedule fits with possible team interaction.

Transition Activities

Brainstorm transition and routine activities occurring after each recess. Some examples are journals, math warm-ups, sentence corrections, sustained silent reading (SSR), and read-alouds. Decide about placement in your daily schedule. If you routinely have a transition activity after each recess, it will allow you time to meet with students as needed, to assess them individually, or to complete preparation for the next activity. These routines should be explicitly taught during the first month so students may practice their expected behavior.

Daily and Weekly Activities

Consider other daily and weekly activities, such as "morning message," calendar, daily agenda, jobs, homework assignments, current events, quizzes, tests, and class meetings. Enter these in your plan book.

You now have a basic daily and weekly schedule. While scheduling your midrange planning, you can add the sequence of activities for each unit and series of lessons.

Certain lessons require more details than others. Consider adding a basic plan structure to your plan book. Another notebook may include more specific plans: for instance, an introduction to the lesson or set, instruction, guided practice, independent practice, and closure. A detailed outline for routine procedures is necessary only for initial teaching, to assist you in planning the routine's procedures, modeling, and practice.

Careful planning does not imply that these are etched in stone. Your students' backgrounds, interests, and needs will drive your instruction. Plans can serve as a road map, but remember: The route may be changed whenever needed!

TABLE 1.6

Time	Monday	Tuesday	Wednesday	Thursday	Friday
8:30-8:45	Journals	Journals	Journals	Journals	Journals
8:45-9:00	Morning Message	Morning Message	Morning Message	Morning Message	Morning Message
9:00-10:00	Literacy	Literacy	Composition Lab	Literacy	Literacy
10:00-10:15	Recess	Recess	Recess	Recess	Recess
10:00-10:20	SSR	SSR	SSR	SSR	SSR
10:20-11:00	Library	Math	Math	Math	Class Meeting

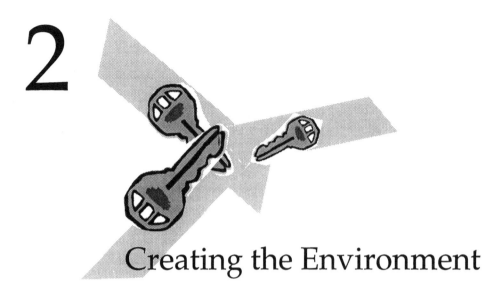

2

Creating the Environment

Organize your classroom in a way that allows for a variety of learning styles and situations and that keeps materials organized and accessible to students.

CHAPTER CONTENTS

◆

ROOM ARRANGEMENT

Environment plays a critical role in the classroom. How you set up your room affects the learning that will take place. Before students arrive, organize your room with an eye toward flexibility in the future.

Following are suggestions for activity areas. If space, furniture, and equipment do not allow setting these up as separate areas, you might rethink the storage of equipment and supplies so an area can be used for more than one center (i.e., an art center might be used as a teacher-directed lesson space if that center is not used during the time block for group instruction.

Center Areas for Kindergarten to Second Grade

Establish noisy and quiet areas in proper proximity: art, blocks, projects, and playhouse in the noisy part of the room; listening center and library corner in the quiet area. Use the following guidelines:

- ☑ Sufficient space for whole-group meetings on the floor (rug area) near a bulletin board—or within easy viewing of a chart stand when writing together
- ☑ Table large enough to work with groups or for teacher-directed small groups (2 tables required if an aide assists with small groups)
- ☑ Art center with supply storage that can be easily accessed by students; if your center includes a table and easels, it can be maintained easier if located near the sink
- ☑ Listening center for 2 to 4 students at a small table or on the floor; center should be equipped with tape recorder, 2 to 4 sets of earphones, and a jack for hooking earphones to the tape recorder
- ☑ Writing center with paper, pens, pencils, crayons, and markers stored in a clearly organized manner
- ☑ Center areas where 2 to 4 students can do independent student activities (e.g., small tables, individual desks, counter space, or floor areas)
- ☑ Library corner with thematic and current-interest books displayed so students may see their covers, plus additional space for a growing collection of student-authored books; also needed: inviting reading space with a comfortable chair, lamp, pillows, and so on (Note: On the first day, *do not* overstock the library. Allow the collection to grow as you read and write books together.)
- ☑ Observation and science area for objects your students bring to share for a particular theme (e.g., shells displayed for a sea life theme or objects with scents displayed for a five-senses theme)
- ☑ Dramatic-play area containing dolls, telephone, dishes, playhouse furniture, plastic food items, and so on; as different themes are studied during the year, this area can be converted to a museum, post office, grocery store, or doctor's office
- ☑ Construction area for blocks, *Legos,* or other manipulatives
- ☑ Computer center

Flexible use of space requires your students to understand *when* it is appropriate to be in a certain area or center. Prepare several Stop Signs or Open-Closed 2-sided signs that can be hung up when a particular center is not available. It is not necessary for each area to be up and running the first day. Area planning allows you to enrich your classroom with materials without rearranging furniture to gain additional space. Train students on how to use each center before allowing independent use. Such training should be a large part of your first month's instruction. Set up centers that are most critical to your instructional goals.

Seating (Dependent on Your Preference)

- Kindergartners need cubbies rather than assigned seating. On the first day, it is not necessary to label cubbies with students' names. During the following few days, they may choose their particular cubby. Having students decorate name cards for their cubbies is a good small-group lesson.
- First and second graders use tables or desks. If tables are used, students need cubbies for storing schoolwork, backpacks, and lunch boxes. First and second graders usually have assigned seats for part of the day, but this arrangement allows for seats to be used in various ways during the day (i.e., reading groups or centers).
- Third- to sixth-grade students may only use desks. Varied seating arrangements can be used, but we recommend that desks be grouped in fours or sixes to encourage cooperation. First-day seating arrangement can be arbitrary, in alphabetical order, or by student choice. As you become familiar with students' behaviors and abilities, you can work together on making changes.

Organization of Supplies

Environment means more than furniture arrangement. Review your materials storage: crayons, glue, scissors, pencils, paper; also games, puzzles, blocks, books, manipulatives, and so on.

Color code and symbol code general supplies so students can become independent when cleaning up. Store supplies in movable tubs or boxes labeled with the same color as the table or work area. Storage area for supplies should be labeled with the same color or shape. Example: If general supplies are needed in five areas, label each with a piece of laminated construction paper cut in these shapes: orange rectangle, red circle, green triangle, yellow square, blue oval. Then, label five supply tubs (containing pencils, crayons, scissors, and glue or paste) with corresponding shapes. Last, label the area to return supplies with those same five shapes. Now, students can easily find and return supplies as needed. Other items used by students on a regular basis, such as puzzles, math manipulatives, games, *Legos,* and so on, can be stored consistently on shelves labeled with their names.

ENVIRONMENT CHECKLIST

- ☑ Many types of fiction and nonfiction books are available. Start with a few, then add to your collection during the coming weeks. Younger children return to familiar books, and they read with greater concentration. Add to your collection of read-aloud books.
- ☑ Establish an inviting library corner. Students should have access to cassette tapes or CD-ROMs that accompany books.
- ☑ Have reading material other than books available (magazines, catalogues, and cards). Videos and CD-ROMs are also available.
- ☑ Include creative materials to enable students to express their own personal interpretations in project form.
- ☑ Make opportunities and materials available for students to conduct research and experiments.
- ☑ Allocate spaces for oral activities (Readers' Theater, choral speaking, and playacting) that will not interfere with silent reading and listening activities.
- ☑ Provide blank cassette tapes for students to record or listen to their "story readings," or both.
- ☑ Establish quiet corners for students to write, read, dream, and think.
- ☑ Hang bulletin boards to display students' work, allow for learning and interaction; support what is taught.
- ☑ Space should be neatly organized and designed for easy maintenance by the class community.
- ☑ The classroom should provide opportunities for students to choose from several activities and places or ways to work.

PREPARATION PRIOR TO THE FIRST DAY

Prepare the following before students arrive:

K-6 Class List

This includes all students' addresses, bus routes and stops, and telephone numbers. New students should be added to the list immediately. Refer to a map or take a tour of your attendance area to become familiar with neighborhoods and bus stops. Obtain this information from your school secretary or a veteran teacher, or ask them to be your tour guide (or both). Start by organizing your list in alphabetical order by *first name*. The school's list is prepared by *last* name. As you will be concentrating on learning students' first names, use of the school's list will slow you down. Also, students' given names are not necessarily what they use; for instance, if María Guadalupe is called Lupita, you'll become confused. Creating your own list is worth the effort.

A computer database is an efficient way to create a class list. Many types of integrated software are available: *AppleWorks, Microsoft Office, Microsoft Works,* and so on. Making changes and correcting errors becomes easier. Also, the database can be used to create labels for a substitute's field trips, bus transportation name tags, and so on.

K-6 Bus Tags and Bus List

Carefully research how your students will get home. Know their bus routes and stops, who will be picked up and by whom, and who will walk home and with whom. For younger students, this information is critical—you do not want to lose a student! Ask how to obtain this information from the school secretary or a veteran teacher at your grade level, then,

- ☑ Create a master bus list (in alphabetical order by first name) to be kept on a clipboard and carried with you to the bus lines.
- ☑ Prepare a *how we get home* graph, matching students to their respective buses. Post as a wall display for reference at dismissal time. (Creating this graph with students on the first day is a good opening day, whole-group activity.)
- ☑ Prepare individual bus tags with students' first and last names, home address, phone number (optional), and bus route and stop. (If using a database, use the *Print Merge* option for address labels that include this information. Printed address labels equate to instant, easy-to-stick-on bus tags that may be prepared daily and reflect any class changes).
- ☑ Depending on students' age and their bus driver's needs, some students wear bus tags for the first 2 weeks. Younger children need tags longer than older students. Bus drivers carry an enormous responsibility in making sure that students arrive home safely. Ask what is required of you so their jobs can run more smoothly.
- ☑ Decide if students should return their bus tags daily. If so, laminate the tags, and they can become lasting necklaces. Often, there are several students who do not return theirs and require new tags. Decide which is best: a master tag that can be copied onto address labels, printing new tags each time for all students, OR making new tags for those few students when needed. Decide on a time and procedure for figuring out who needs new tags. Remember to plan a time to make new tags each day.

K-6 Name Tags for Permanent Seats

Name tags can be prepared prior to the first day, or you might have students create name cards for their own permanent seats. One "first-days" goal is to build a sense of community and inclusion. Creating a climate where community members are known by name is an important part of this goal. The more ways that students can create their own communities, including working together on individual name cards, the better.

K-2 Name Tags

Wearable name tags must be prepared for each student. During the first day, one of your most important tasks will be to learn their names. The more visual information available, the faster names can be learned. Some schools have a high transiency rate, meaning that the list you receive before the first day may be inaccurate. Ask a veteran teacher or school secretary if this might occur at your site. If so, choose a tag style that can easily be changed or discarded.

Name tags can represent the special shape or character of your first theme. Create these from sturdy paper, laminated for use over several days. Attach roving or string to make necklaces—or you may purchase plastic holders affixed with a pin, clip, or string. These are inexpensive and available at office supply stores. Write names on the cards, add a sticker, then slip into the plastic holder. These tags will survive the school year, can be available for a substitute's use, and are easily changed when a student leaves or arrives. When forming temporary groups for first-week activities, color code the name tags using different colors of roving or varied stickers. Students with the same color roving or sticker are placed in the same group. Collect name tags at day's end; replace with a bus tag, if appropriate.

In K-1, students might read the names each day as a whole group. One of the first things students learn to read is each other's names. Making this a routine provides many opportunities for teaching phonics in context.

K-6: Calendar. The classroom calendar should be up and ready to go. This calendar and its related activities constitute a routine you want to establish. It is relatively easy to get together and can be a 10- to 20-minute activity done every day. See the section on the calendar routine in Chapter 2 for how to set one up.

K-2: Preselected Read-Alouds. These should be short, with good illustrations and predictable, repetitive text. Having these preselected and within easy reach of the whole-group area will help with those moments that need to be filled. See the section on read-alouds in Chapter 9 for a bibliography.

3-6: Preselected Read-Alouds. Books that you really enjoy and that will capture the interest of your students make reading aloud an enjoyable part of the day.

K-2: Written List of Fingerplays and Songs. You should memorize and be ready with a repertoire of at least 10 songs and fingerplays. See Chapter 5 for some easy ones. Student attention is more easily and gently gained through chanting and singing than through overt phrases, such as "I need your attention." If you start a chant, soon all the students will join in.

K-6: Lesson Plan Book. Set up your plan book with dates for the year (look at a school calendar and put the starting and ending dates of the weeks of school at the top of the pages in your plan book and list all holidays). At the first teachers' meeting, you will probably receive various other important dates to remember. If you have your plan book set up, you can immediately transfer those important dates and responsibilities into your book so you don't forget them. The following are some examples:

- Yard duty for each week (this is important—put this right next to the date at the top of the page in red ink)
- Back-to-School Night

☑ Parent conferences
☑ Vacation days
☑ Staff Development Training
☑ Vision and hearing screenings
☑ Special events
☑ Testing schedule
☑ Report card deadlines
☑ Release time

Having the schedule set up ahead of time will relieve you of trying to find that calendar of events in your piles of papers. This is a good habit to get into: Every time you receive a piece of paper in your box with an important date, you have a place to write it down where you will remember to look at it!

When you set up your plan book, leave a space or column for a "things to do and places to go" list. List your major preparation here. Also list meeting times and places, so you don't forget them.

K-6: File Folder for Each Student. Write each student's name on a file folder, and alphabetize the folders by first names. Have the files easily accessible in an open box or tub. Keep extra folders on hand for new arrivals. Having your folders ready will enable you to quickly file those beginning-of-the-year activities that you want to save (e.g., self-portraits, writing samples, teacher observations, parent notes).

K-6: Homework Tub or System. Set up a tub where students put their homework, notes from home, permission and other forms, and the like. Keep this in a consistent place near the door.

1-6: Individual Work Folders. Make each student a construction-paper folder labeled with his or her name. All daily work can be corrected or checked and filed. These folders should be kept in a central location, not in individual student desks. All work can be compiled and sent home on Friday or Monday for review and signature by parents. This provides 1 night a week of homework and the opportunity for parents to see their children's progress over a week's time.

K-6: Bulletin Boards. Create a learning environment that is interesting, inviting, and comfortable. Bulletin boards should reflect the atmosphere you want to have in your classroom.

☑ Leave at least 1 blank board for the display of an initial classroom project.
☑ Plan a welcome-type bulletin board (e.g., "Famous Fourth Graders": put up pictures, names, interview information).
☑ Use your bulletin boards to tie into the beginning-of-the-year themes.

Many districts have teacher centers where you can use a die-cut machine to cut the letters that you need for bulletin boards. Teacher supply stores also may have prepackaged commercial bulletin boards that would fit in. Remember, however, that to obtain maximum advantage from bulletin boards, you should involve students in the design, layout, and especially the content.

ESSENTIAL KNOWLEDGE

Be sure you know how to find the following:

- ☑ Classroom key
- ☑ Classroom light switch
- ☑ Classroom heat control
- ☑ Intercom

Academics

- ☑ Cumulative records
- ☑ Diagnostic and placement tests
- ☑ Grade book
- ☑ Grade-level and subject expectations
- ☑ Library books, texts, workbooks
- ☑ Plan book
- ☑ Profiles, individual records
- ☑ Report cards
- ☑ Science and math manipulatives
- ☑ Standardized test results
- ☑ Student and home information

Equipment and Machinery

- ☑ Computers, diskettes, printer, paper
- ☑ Cooking wares, stove
- ☑ Desks, chairs, tables
- ☑ Ditto machine, thermal machine, *Risograph*
- ☑ Easels, chalkboards
- ☑ Electrical outlets
- ☑ Film projector, screen, extension cords
- ☑ Films, slides, videos
- ☑ Filmstrip projector
- ☑ Filmstrips
- ☑ Laminator
- ☑ Overhead projector
- ☑ Overhead projector pens and plastics
- ☑ Pencil sharpener
- ☑ Photocopier, photocopier key

- ☑ Slide projector
- ☑ Tape recorder
- ☑ Video equipment and supplies

Personnel (Name, Schedule, Location)

- ☑ Aide(s)
- ☑ Cafeteria staff
- ☑ Custodians
- ☑ Fellow teachers
- ☑ GATE (Gifted and Talented Education) staff
- ☑ Migrant personnel
- ☑ Nurse
- ☑ Secretary, office personnel
- ☑ Special education staff
- ☑ Speech specialists
- ☑ Yard duty staff

Procedures

- ☑ Abuse and neglect reporting
- ☑ Bus rules and procedures
- ☑ Cafeteria rules
- ☑ Class rules
- ☑ Evacuation of building
- ☑ Field trips
- ☑ Fire or disaster plan
- ☑ Fire extinguisher
- ☑ Library and hall passes
- ☑ Location of all schedules
- ☑ Lunch money, tickets, charges
- ☑ Petty cash
- ☑ Phone procedures
- ☑ Playground rules
- ☑ Power outage
- ☑ Roll sheet
- ☑ Seating chart
- ☑ Student or aide illness
- ☑ Substitutes: number, plans
- ☑ Supply and purchase orders
- ☑ Weekly bulletin

Supplies

- ☑ Art supplies
- ☑ Chalk, chalkboard erasers

- ☑ Cleaning supplies: broom, dustpan, sponge, soap
- ☑ Clipboards
- ☑ Crayons
- ☑ Ditto and thermal masters
- ☑ Envelopes
- ☑ File folders
- ☑ First-aid kit
- ☑ Hole punch
- ☑ Kleenex
- ☑ Label-making gun and tape
- ☑ P.E. equipment: whistle, stopwatch
- ☑ Paper: butcher, construction, ditto, scratch, writing, tagboard
- ☑ Paper clips
- ☑ Paper towels
- ☑ Paste, glue
- ☑ Pencils, erasers, pens
- ☑ Pins
- ☑ Post-it Notes
- ☑ Rubber bands
- ☑ Rulers
- ☑ Scissors
- ☑ Staplers, staples
- ☑ Stickers
- ☑ Tape: Scotch, masking
- ☑ White board and dry-erase markers, erasers

3

Daily Routines and Procedures

Consistent daily routines will help students feel comfortable and know what to expect. Clear procedures will help students know exactly what behavior is expected in the various learning situations you create.

CHAPTER CONTENTS

CARDINAL RULES OF CLASSROOM MANAGEMENT

Remember the cardinal rules of classroom management: *Model, practice, focus on the positive,* and *be consistent!!*

The following sections outline procedures for various classroom management areas that must be in place for you to be successful. These are the "hidden systems" you may not have been aware of in your observations of classrooms or in your student teaching. We urge you to read them carefully, implement them as outlined, and keep at it until your students have learned them.

Creating procedures helps you think through your behavioral expectations for any given activity. That way, you are able to communicate those expectations clearly to the students and thus prevent disruptions. You can either tell the students your expectations for a specific procedure or have the class develop them under your guidance.

FREEZE AND LISTEN

This is a must. You need to decide what signal you will use to notify your students that they must stop, look, and listen to an adult. This could be a bell, a chord on the piano, a note sounded on a xylophone, a hand signal—whatever you choose. In kindergarten and first grade, it is useful to have the students do an accompanying body motion when they hear the signal (e.g., hands in the air, hands on head).

Starting from the first day, at the first transition, you must model, role-play, and practice this procedure over and over. It is critical that all the adults in the room model the desired behavior along with the students. At the first class meeting, explain the procedure—a visual is helpful (e.g., a picture of a bell, above a stop sign, above big eyes, above big ears) to use as you explain (see Figure 3.1). At the first whole-group meeting, you might do the following to model the procedure (note that the language in this example is designed for a K-2 class; you will need to adapt it for grades 3 to 6).

Figure 3.1. Sample Freeze-and-Listen

Say, "Today, we're going to practice what we do when we hear this sound. First, Alicia [the teacher's aide] and I will show you what to do." You then choose a child to be the "teacher" and whisper in his or her ear what he or she is to do—for example, let you talk and color for a few moments, and then ring a bell. You pretend to be coloring and talking with Alicia until your "teacher" rings the bell or gives whatever freeze-and-listen signal you have chosen. At that point, you must model exactly what you want the kids to do: *Freeze* and *look at the "teacher."*

Next, call up a small group of students to role-play what you and your aide just did. Your aide can take the role-play group away to review what they are going to do while you give the others the task of being the observers and watching for the proper behavior. Have the role-players pretend to be busy.

Make your freeze-and-listen signal, and *praise, praise, praise* when they comply. Encourage the audience to praise also.

Now, you're ready to have the whole class role-play. Have them stay in the circle and pretend to be busy coloring, talking quietly to their neighbors. Make your freeze-and-listen signal. Your aide should be instructed to go to noncompliers and quietly remind them of the procedure. You should focus on giving positive praise to those who are complying and to the whole class when all comply.

Review the procedure with the students using the visual. This activity should take 10 to 15 minutes and should be followed by something active.

This procedure will have to be practiced often—at every transition, for the first week or so. That means you should continue to have your aide or parent volunteer involved, continue to praise, and continue to redirect those students having a hard time learning the procedure. Spending time and energy putting this procedure firmly in place will pay huge dividends later.

CLEANUP

In an active, interactive classroom, your students must be responsible for the maintenance of the environment. Several different types of cleanup need to be considered.

Individual responsibilities. The rule is to clean up after yourself. During the first few days of school, include this in any modeling you do. For example, if you are doing a cut-and-paste art project and are explaining the how to, be sure to include the how to of cleanup in your explanation—where to put your scissors when you've finished, where scraps go, and so on. As you review the project after completion, make special note to compliment the students' efforts at cleanup. In kindergarten and first grade, it is effective to start a chant or song to accompany cleanup. For example, to the tune of "The Farmer in the Dell," you can sing, "It's time to clean up, it's time to clean up. Heigh ho the derry-o, it's time to clean up. Es hora de limpiar, es hora de limpiar. Que viva la escuela, es hora de limpiar."

The success of cleanup will depend on your having clearly marked areas for supplies that are easily accessible to the students. Remember the decisions you made about materials. Make sure the students know their responsibilities. Students must know what to do after they have cleaned up their own work spaces (e.g., sit at the whole-group area and wait quietly or go to their seat and look at a book).

Classroom responsibilities. These cleanup duties involve such tasks as keeping the book corner neat, washing the tables, and taking the roll to the office. It is helpful to have a "jobs chart" that lists the tasks that need to be done on a daily basis but in which not everyone needs to participate. Such a chart could take many different forms (a sample format is shown in Figure 3.2); however, the most important aspects are that students are trained in what the jobs entail, that jobs are rotated in a fair manner, and that you are consistent in making students accountable for completing their jobs. Some possible classroom jobs for

Figure 3.2. Jobs Chart

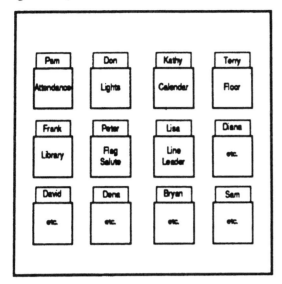

students are library monitor, light monitor, office monitor, leader of cleanup, leader of games, leader for the flag salute, pencils monitor, and line leader.

The students can participate in the development of the jobs chart by brainstorming what jobs need to be done. Don't do this the first day of school but shortly thereafter. Again, role-play, model, and reinforce what is expected for each job. This could be done as an inclusion activity in which you divide the class into groups and have each group learn one job and teach it to a partner.

Special project cleanup responsibilities. When you plan a messy activity, consider how you can involve the students in cleanup. Often, the cleanup of these projects can fall to you or your aide. Include cleanup procedures in the explanation of the project and review them with students before beginning to work on the project.

PROCEDURES FOR LESSONS, GROUPS, AND ROTATIONS

Teacher-Directed Whole-Class Lesson

Procedures for a teacher-directed lesson with the whole class may vary depending on the kind of lesson involved. You may want to require that desks are cleared off or that certain materials are out on the desks. Use your freeze-and-listen signal to get attention.

You want to have clear procedures for the kind of attention you expect (chairs turned to face you, eyes looking at you, students may be drawing while you are talking, or whatever). Think them through, and make them clear and reasonable (for example, consider what to tell students to do if they can't see or hear you or if they need to sharpen a pencil). Spell the procedures out clearly.

Use positive language when writing your procedures. Say what you *want* the students to do, not what they shouldn't do ("Listen quietly" instead of "Don't talk"). Make the procedures short (use as few words as needed to get the information across), and make them few in number. Write them on a chart, and keep them on hand to refer to. Now you're ready to teach the procedures to the class. Discuss each one, model what it looks like, and show what it doesn't look like. Reinforce the procedures using positive praise. The use of thoughtfully worded and clearly taught procedures is the foundation to your classroom management.

Rules and *procedures* are not the same things. Rules apply to all students all of the time. "Be respectful," "Use your words, not your fists," and "No toys or candy at school" are all examples of rules. Whether it's during reading centers or a math lesson, the rules do not change. Procedures, on the other hand, vary according to the lesson or activity. "Raise your hand and wait to be called on" is a good procedure for a teacher-led lesson but not for paired interviews.

Sample Procedure Chart for a Teacher-Directed Whole-Class Lesson

1. Clear desk and stay in your seat.
2. One person talks at a time.
3. Raise your hand to speak.
4. Focus on (look at!) the speaker.
5. Follow teacher directions.

---

1. Quita todo de encima de tu escritorio y quédate en tu asiento.
2. Sólo una persona habla a la vez.
3. Levanta la mano para hablar.
4. Fíjate en el orador. (Mírale al orador.)
5. Sigue las instrucciones de la maestra.

Tailoring Instruction for English Language Learners (ELL)

Students who learn English benefit from a variety of opportunities when natural language becomes connected to meaning. Meaning can be conveyed easily through pictures, actions, and explicit situations; for example, when handing someone a ball say, *Go play ball.*

The Following Examples Demonstrate How Teachers Bring Meaning to Their Lessons:

☑ Exaggerate gestures, facial expressions, and voice intonation.
☑ Limit sentence length and complexity; pause at the end of each sentence.
☑ Speak slowly, enunciate new vocabulary, pause after new words, and use synonyms.
☑ At the start of a lesson, define key words using familiar language.
☑ Clarify meaning; use pictures, props, motions, context clues, simpler words.
☑ Repeat, emphasize, and paraphrase key concepts.
☑ Summarize main ideas frequently.

Ask yourself, Does my lesson include a variety of strategies to help ELL students learn language and understand the lesson's context?

Questioning Strategies

Use questioning strategies often to ensure that students understand content and gain skill in using language. Questions should not be set up as a test but as an opportunity to practice language. Questioning strategies should be adapted to the students' language ability. Students with stronger English skills will need less support for their responses. Mixed groups require questioning strategies at every level, allowing opportunities for all to participate. Following are questions adapted for the stages used in English learning, starting with the earliest:

Hardly any English:

☑ Ask questions your students can answer by moving their bodies. Model the expected behavior.

If your dress is red, stand up: *Are you wearing a red dress?* Model: stand up.

Do you think the bears will find Goldilocks? Show a thumb up for *yes,* thumb down for *no.*

Beginning speech emerging:

☑ Ask questions requiring short 1-, 2-, or 3-word answers. Model the responses.

Where will Goldilocks go next: to the chair or to bed? (Point to illustrations as questions are asked).

☑ Model sentence frames for students to practice and use in response to your questions:

What would you do with $100? Model several times: *If I had $100, I would buy a new bike* or *if I had $100, I would buy a video game. What would you buy?*

Intermediate English skill level:

☑ Build on student responses for modeling focus language patterns:

Mario says, *I like soccer and football.* Teacher expands, *Mario likes to play soccer, and he likes to play football. Sara, what do you like to play?*

☑ Ask confirmation questions frequently. Before responding in the large group, have students pair and share.

More advanced level:

☑ Ask students to repeat, paraphrase, or clarify what you or another student has said, enabling the sharing of information.

Ask yourself: Have my questions allowed all students, whatever their English language proficiency, to participate in our discussion?

The following strategies maximize student learning for all but are crucial to ELL students:

Build Lesson Backgrounds by Proceeding From Known to Unknown

During the first months of school, learn as much as possible about each student's family, home life, and community. Use concept maps to determine what students know about a topic by first placing the topic at the center of the page. Have students brainstorm their knowledge of the topic. Enter their responses. Feed new concepts into the map.

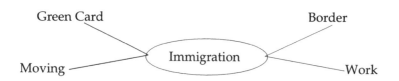

Ask yourself: Does my lesson take students from WHAT they know to what I WANT them to know?

Personalized Lessons

Students focus on lessons relating to their personal experiences—most specifically, themselves. Make a special effort to combine their world with each lesson:

- Draw examples from your students' experiences.
- Use pictures, books, and movies representing a variety of ethnic backgrounds.
- Use analogies relating new concepts to students' familiar experiences.

Ask yourself: Has each student been personally involved in the lesson?

Maximize Interaction

Students learn language when actively engaged in a lesson and more from peers than from their teacher. Provide opportunities for interaction within lessons. Working one-on-one with others and in small cooperative groups also fosters language development.

- Add songs, poems, and chants to reinforce the lesson's language.
- Before asking students to respond in a large group, provide opportunities for them to share with a buddy.
- Structure cooperative learning groups so all students have the opportunity to discuss things and share different roles within the group.

Ask yourself: Have I provided a variety of ways for students to interact with material used in the lesson?

Preview Lessons Orally

Previewing helps ELL students get beyond the mechanical difficulties of reading, enabling them to concentrate on lesson content. When previewing a lesson,

- Lead students sequentially through the chapter or lesson by outlining the primary concepts.
- Familiarize students with new vocabulary and idioms of the lesson.
- Connect language to illustrations.
- Discuss charts or graphs so that students learn to change graphic representation into language.
- Use the following strategies to combine student experience with your lesson: modeling, visuals, pictures, questioning, paraphrasing, restating, gesturing, and dramatic representation.

Ask yourself: Has important content been conveyed and key vocabulary emphasized so that ELL students will understand the story when read aloud to them?

Use Visuals, Graphic Organizers, and Hands-On Activities

Visuals, including those created by students, enhance their understanding of a concept:

- Graphic organizers help students arrange information. These may include charts, tables, diagrams, and graphs as well as concept maps for brainstorming/organizing information.
- Matrices, Venn diagrams, and other graphic organizing structures also help show relationships between information.
- Hands-on activities include experimentation, measuring, cutting, charting, weighing, and so on and involve students more actively in the learning process. All students should share tools equally.

Ask yourself: Have I chosen appropriate visuals and graphic organizers to help students envision the lesson content?

Use of Effective Literature for English Language Learners

Quality literature and picture books are excellent tools for helping ELL students develop language and concepts. These suggestions assist in using books effectively with all students, including ELL learners.

How do you choose a book?

- Read the entire book aloud to yourself.
- Choose one with illustrations that match the text.

- ☑ Use picture books with all age levels.
- ☑ Find books that contain clear examples of what you are attempting to teach.
- ☑ Make minimal use of idiomatic expressions.
- ☑ Find books that are large enough for students to see.
- ☑ Use books with simple sentence construction.
- ☑ Find books that can be read in 5 to 10 minutes.
- ☑ Select books that can be read again and again.
- ☑ Look for repetitive or patterned language with opportunities for choral responses.

How to Introduce a Book for ELL Students
That Determines Background Knowledge

- ☑ Set a purpose for reading, such as focusing on story structure (beginning, middle, and end) or language structure (e.g., past tense: *he walked to the store, he looked in the window*). Explain what they should do with this book. As you read the book aloud, model expected responses.
- ☑ Show the cover, read the title aloud, then ask, *What do you know about it?* Or give a brief preview, asking for predictions.
- ☑ Picture-walk. Flip through a few pages slowly, then ask, *What did you notice?*
- ☑ Preview idiomatic or difficult *content* words. Example: If the book is about a sorcerer, ask what students know about magic. As they share their schema related to magic, you can add the fact that one of the names for a magician is *sorcerer*.
- ☑ Think through what language/content you wish to use from the book. Your choice of activity helps students gain skills and knowledge from their experience with the book.

Focus on the Text's Language Structures and Vocabulary

- ☑ Imagine yourself as a second-language learner. Seek words or language structures that make the key point of the story difficult to understand. To get the meaning across, consider synonyms or gestures, intonation, hand movements, and use of illustrations.
- ☑ Create opportunities for helping students remember difficult vocabulary. Pictures can be drawn to illustrate nouns; motions may be used for verbs.
- ☑ Language games help in learning complex language constructions. Example: For the grammatical construction, "Would have done, could have done, should have done," make up chants/games for students to practice construction. *Who stole the cookies from the cookie jar?* is an example of a chanting game used to practice language and can be adapted for other language structures.
- ☑ Find opportunities for choral responses: You ask the question, model the response, and have all repeat the response together. Have students fill in the blanks for oral responses, hand motions, sound effects, or gestures (e.g., thumbs up).

Reading the Book

- ☑ Turn the book so students can see the pictures.

☑ Become an actor: Read slowly, but with expression; use your voice intonation to convey meaning. Track the print with your finger. Stop at key words and phrases and display the picture. Find opportunities for students to respond or interact with the text.

☑ Look at your students' faces frequently to determine if they are following you. Repeat questions to check who understands and who does not.

☑ Do not turn book sharing into a *listening* test. You are modeling reading while providing interactive opportunities for students to become involved in the book.

Ask yourself: As I read this book aloud, are my students engaged in ways that will further their learning of language?

Teacher-Directed Whole Group on the Floor or Rug

In kindergarten, most whole-group instruction is done with the students sitting on the floor. In first and second grade, this is still true, but some instruction is done with students sitting at their seats. For this type of instruction, see the procedures outlined earlier.

For whole-group floor procedures, the following should be practiced from the first day of school:

☑ Students should know where and how to sit. Some teachers prefer a circle arrangement. If you choose this arrangement, mark the circle on the floor with tape to delineate its size and where students should sit.

☑ Some teachers prefer a group with an undefined shape or rows. If you use rows, again, mark the rug or floor with tape. For an undefined arrangement, you need to delineate the boundaries of the group space in some way—often, furniture will do this, but you must make it clear to your students what is out of bounds (e.g., being under a piece of furniture or behind a chair).

☑ It is important to practice the "how to" of sitting on the floor. Don't use the term *Indian style*—avoid stereotyping. Instead, show the students the cross-legged position expected at floor time. Use a chant such as "I sit on the floor by myself, crisscross" to remind them of the expectation instead of singling out individuals. Again, use your aide to individually help those having a hard time.

☑ Decide and tell your students how you expect them to respond to questions or to join in discussions—raise hands, shout out, wait until someone has finished speaking, or whatever. This may vary from activity to activity but should be made clear at the beginning of each activity.

Small-Group Teacher-Directed Lesson

In this format, the teacher will be working with a small group while the rest of the class is working either independently or in other small groups with learning assistants (adults or cross-age helpers), cooperatively, or whatever. Before working with a small group, set the rules for the other groups in the class—what if they need to use the bathroom, don't have a pencil, or have a question? All problems should have procedures so that, short of a minor disaster, you are free to work with your small group.

In your small group, set procedures for how students are to come to the work area, what they should bring, what transition activity they are to do while waiting for the directed group to start, how they are to respond in a discussion (informally, raising hands, and so on), and if supplies are at the workstation, who distributes them, who collects them, and what procedures are to be followed in leaving the workstation.

Sample Procedure Chart for a Small-Group Teacher-Directed Lesson

1. Come quietly to group with materials.
2. Follow directions on board for transition activity.
3. Give attention to speaker in the group.
4. Raise hand to speak unless it's open discussion.
5. Clean up before leaving.
6. Return quietly to your own seat and begin work.

1. Ven calladito a tu grupo con tus materiales.
2. Sigue las direcciones en el pizarrón para la actividad transitoria.
3. Fija tu atención en el orador del grupo.
4. Levanta la mano para hablar a menos de que sea una discusión abierta.
5. Limpia la estación.
6. Regresa calladito a tu propio escritorio y comienza a trabajar.

Small-Group Rotations

Usually, a teacher sets up some kind of rotation system to ensure that he or she sees each student on a regular basis and has the opportunity to provide direct instruction to small groups. It is critical to train your students in the rotation system you choose before doing any in-depth content.

You need to think through the organization of any rotation times you will schedule. For example, during an hour-long language arts period, you might want to see 2 groups for 1 half hour each. That would mean that in a class with 4 groups, you would see each student every other day. Or you may wish to see each group every day. Therefore, you would need a 2-hour block for language arts or would see each group for only 15 minutes. Once you have decided for how long you will see each group, you have other decisions to make:

- What kind of adult help do you have? What will their responsibilities be? What kind of system will you use to tell them what to do?
- How will the students be grouped: by language, by ability, heterogeneously by language?
- What will the non-teacher-directed activities be: journals, spelling, workbooks, handwriting, listening center, oral reading?

☑ Will you use cross-age tutors? What activities are appropriate for them to work with?

☑ Will students always rotate with the same groups, or will they be divided differently for independent workstations?

☑ Where will you meet with students? Where will the aides, tutors, and parent volunteers meet with students?

Once you have made these decisions, you can begin to formulate a plan. Sit down with a piece of paper, a class list, and your assessment information, if you wish. On a blank piece of paper, make a grid with the number of rotations you will have down one side and the activities you have across the top. For example,

	Teacher Aide Directed Lesson	Independent Cut and Paste Game	Listening Book and Tape
8:30-9:00			
9:00-9:30			
9:30-10:00			
10:00-10:30			

This would be a 4-group rotation, with the teacher seeing each student every day. Once you have your time schedule and activities down, you can begin to group your students. We recommend heterogeneous grouping as opposed to skill-level grouping.

In a bilingual situation, the only limitation during a language arts time will be language of instruction. You will need to have your students in groups based on whether they are learning literacy concepts in English or Spanish. In math, social studies, and other subjects, however, languages may be mixed.

Divide your class as nearly as you can into 4 equally numbered groups. Name each group (number, color, animal; see Table 3.1). This is just for the purposes of figuring out the rotation. Once groups have been established, a good team-building activity is for them to name themselves. You can then begin to fill in the rotation scheme.

What colors would go in the listening column in Table 3.1? If you thought Green, Blue, Red, and then Yellow, you're on your way to developing systems. This is the simplest system; students stay with the same group throughout the rotation schedule. This is a good place to start.

Now that you know what will happen, you need to teach the rotation and what is expected at each "station." Plan on spending at least 2 weeks being the facilitator in this learning by easing into a full rotation system. In other words, don't plan to spend time with your small group—you will be roaming, praising, answering questions, keeping students on task, and so on. You will only be frustrated if you try to do a lesson as well. Have independent work for your group to do. The following procedure outlines a sample strategy for introducing rotation centers:

TABLE 3.1
Sample Rotation Grid

	Teacher	Aide	Independent	Listening
8:30-9:00	Blue	Red	Yellow	?
9:00-9:30	Red	Yellow	Green	?
9:30-10:00	Yellow	Green	Blue	?
10:00-10:30	Green	Blue	Red	?

- Prepare a chart with the students' names listed under the colors of their groups or written on construction paper of the colors of their groups. Post the chart near your whole-group meeting area. (For kindergartners, you could also add a photocopied picture of each child next to his or her name.)
- Show the chart to the students at whole-group time. Explain to them how to find which group they belong to. Have several students come up and point to their names. Have the whole group shout out these students' group colors.
- Say, "All students in the Blue Group stand up quietly." Read off the names from your chart and have the students sit down as you call their names. Continue for each group. (In kindergarten, hand out colored-yarn necklaces for the students to wear as they determine their group colors. You can use these for a few days to help you and the students learn the groups.)

Now, hopefully, everyone knows his or her group. The next step is to work on the rotation scheme. Shorten the time allotted at each station during the first 2 weeks of practice. A sample strategy follows:

- On the first day of practice, have all your students learn what happens at the teacher center. Say, "When it's your turn to work with me, you will come to the horseshoe table in the back of the classroom. While you wait for me to get everyone settled, you will look at one of the books in the blue box." Have one group role-play this for the whole class.
- Next, move everyone to the next station. Say, "This is where you will work with Alicia [aide]." Explain all items the students should bring with them when coming to this work area, if any. Move through all the stations in this manner. Do it quickly—only an overview at this time.
- Now, introduce a rotation chart, such as the one shown in Figure 3.3, or an individual "map" to be pasted in each student's work folder, such as those shown in Figure 3.4. In whole group, have the students determine where they go for Rotation 1. At your signal, the Blue Group will go to its assigned area, followed by the Red, Green, and Yellow groups, one at a time. When all groups are at their assigned first rota-

Figure 3.3. Rotation Chart

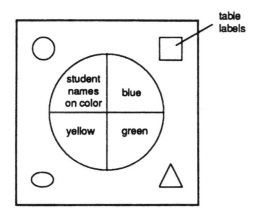

tions, make your freeze-and-listen signal. Wait for complete attention, and then have students determine where they go for the second rotation. Model how to rotate: Walk quietly and quickly to where you go. Do this all together by saying, "Everyone stand up. Point to where you go. Now, walk quietly to Rotation 2." Repeat for Rotations 3 and 4. Give plenty of praise and encouragement.

☑ Now that students are at Rotation 4, have them go back to Rotation 1, and have an activity planned for them to do.

☑ The next day, review the rotation scheme in whole group. Use 4 students from each of the 4 groups to model. Start with Rotation 1. Have the 4 role-play students go to their assigned tables, and have the other students help you review the signal that will tell them to move. Make the signal and say, "Rotation 2." The role-play students should move accordingly. Other students can applaud. Continue role-playing with Rotations 3 and 4.

☑ Now, you're ready to do a full-scale run. Have group activities prepared and at the centers. Activities should be simple. Remember that your small-group activity should be independent. The more responsibility you can give to your students for figuring out what to do, the better. For example, a directions poster for each center will give them visual clues as to what to do. Directions should rely on pictures and words to get the message across.

☑ Encourage your students to ask each other for help. *Do not allow yourself to become the sole keeper of knowledge. Be consistent in not answering the questions that students can ask each other.* Explain to your students that when they have questions, they should first ask themselves, then a friend, before they raise their hands to let you know they have questions. Stress the importance of not interrupting the teacher when he or she is teaching. This is part of developing a love for learning—the most important element in the classroom is having respect for that process.

☑ Dismiss each group in turn to go to Rotation 1. You should roam and give specific praise, help any students who are having a hard time getting started, reinforce work behavior, and so on.

☑ When it is time to move to Rotation 2, make your freeze-and-listen signal. Review cleanup, where they will move, and so on. Say, "You have 2 minutes to clean up and be ready to move. I will know you're ready to move when I see your whole group sitting quietly with folders in front of you and your eyes on me." Wait until you see that. Then, have everyone get up and move to the next station.

☑ Repeat for Rotations 3 and 4. You will probably need to do this for the entire first week. The goal is to establish this routine clearly so you do not need to be involved and can devote your attention to your small group without interruption. You can expect to be able to do this only if you practice, practice, practice the first few weeks of school.

Figure 3.4. Individual Student Rotation "Maps"

	John (Blue group)		
Rotation	Where		
1	Teacher	□
2	Independent	△
3	Aide	○
4	Listening	○

	María (Red group)		
Rotation	Where		
1	Independent	□
2	Aide	△
3	Listening	○
4	Teacher	○

☑ In kindergarten and first grade, putting a soothing record on facilitates calm when returning to whole-group work.

Independent Workers

Spend several weeks training students on independent work. Think through exactly what behaviors will be acceptable during independent work time, and write up a chart explaining these. For instance, will you allow students to talk, to get out of their seats, to ask others for help? What if they need help to sharpen a pencil, get a drink of water, or go to the bathroom? What do they do when they finish their work? Set the procedures, and leave yourself free to monitor behavior. This means that if you're practicing independent time and they need help, you do not help them; instead, you have them follow the procedures that are set up. The following chart has examples of procedures.

Sample Procedure Chart for Independent Workers

1. Work by yourself or with a partner.
2. Focus on the assigned work.
3. Whisper if you need to ask a question.
4. Follow cooperative group procedures if you have a question: (a) Ask yourself, (b) ask a neighbor, (c) ask someone at another table.
5. Do not interrupt the teacher.

---

1. Trabaja sólo o con un(a) compañero/a.
2. Fíjate en el trabajo asignado.
3. Usa voz baja si necesitas hacer una pregunta.
4. Sigue el proceso de grupos cooperativos si tienes alguna pregunta: (a) Pregúntate, (b) pregúntale a un vecino, (c) pregúntale a alguien en otra mesa.
5. No le interrumpas a la maestra.

Cooperative Learning Groups

Teach a *zero-noise hand signal* before beginning any cooperative groups. When you raise your hand, students are to (a) raise their hands, (b) get quiet, and (c) tap the shoulders of others around them to get quiet. Practice this many times throughout the day over several days before beginning cooperative learning groups.

Positive praise. Teach words for use in praising one another. Brainstorm words on the board so that students have words of their own to use. Add to the list throughout the year. Keep the list handy for students to refer to. Role-play, practice, and reward usage of praise words.

Individual and group rewards. Students will continue to need to be rewarded for individual efforts as well as for group efforts. They should receive rewards for processes, procedures, and activities, as well as for products. Rewards can be anything from verbal praise, smiles, and pats on the back to points, raffles, and other tangible rewards. See the section on reward systems.

Cooperative work should include (a) "class-building" activities to build class unity, (b) group- or team-building activities, and (c) partner activities. Having students work in pairs is an effective way to introduce content-packed activities, such as reading, writing, research, or math work, in a cooperative approach.

During the first month of school, teacher attention during cooperative activities should be focused on the procedures and interactions, *not on content*. Processing should occur during each cooperative activity to reflect on what was successful and to generalize the learning to other experiences. Processing questions for a group discussion might include the following:

- Why was your group successful (unsuccessful) in completing the task?
- Did you listen to your group?
- Did you develop any strategy for coming to a decision when people disagreed?
- How could you use that strategy on the playground or at home?

Class Meetings

Class meetings can be used for problem solving, topic discussions, determining class rules, deciding class functions, team-building activities, and positive interactions.

During these meetings, everyone sits in a circle, either on the floor or on chairs, so that all participants can have eye contact. Have the class practice getting into and out of the class-meeting circle (arrange desks, chairs, and so on) following the established procedures. Give students specific praise about what they did well each time. With practice, this should take 1 to 2 minutes.

The students may add items to the agenda as they deem necessary. The location for the agenda should be constant (a section of the chalkboard, a hanging clipboard). Keep minutes of the meeting to refer to. Teach students to make "I" statements, such as "I don't like so much noise during writer's workshop," instead of "John and Benito are talking too much." End with a compliment circle to close the meeting on a positive note. Model effective social skills.

Sample Procedure Chart for Class Meetings

1. Sit with bottoms on the floor (or all 4 legs of chair on floor).
2. Come empty-handed.
3. One person talks at a time; raise your hand to speak.
4. Focus on the speaker.
5. Participate.
6. You have the right to pass on a discussion.
7. Stay in the circle until the meeting is over.

---

1. Siéntate en el suelo (o con las cuatro patas de la silla en el suelo).
2. Deja todo en tu escritorio.
3. Levanta la mano para hablar; sólo una persona habla a la vez.
4. Fíjate en el orador.
5. Participa.
6. Tienes el derecho de no contribuir a la discusión.
7. Quédate en tu lugar en el círculo hasta que la junta termine.

STRATEGIES REGARDING BEHAVIOR

Promoting Good Behavior

If you've put all the previous information in place and still feel your management is not what it should be, we have some additional strategies you might employ:

- ☑ *Use "surprise" reinforcers.* Periodically, without warning, schedule a surprise for your class. Tell them the surprise is a direct result of their good behavior. For example, you might cancel a test, extend PE, have a special art project, or show a video.
- ☑ *Vary your lessons.* Often, disruptions occur because a task took too long. Determine the length of your students' attention span, and plan a change of task. Alternate activities that require large motor movements with those that are quieter.
- ☑ *Build relationships with your students.* Students are more willing to cooperate with people they like. Get to know them as individuals—use plenty of praise. Tell them what they do well. This is particularly effective with students with whom you are having difficulty. Force yourself to find out about those students so you can relate to them on a personal and positive level. Talk about topics they're interested in.
- ☑ *Be a good example.* Model the type of behavior you expect from your students. Model active listening, being prepared, thoughtfulness, and the like. Share your experi-

ences with your students. Tell them how you've handled personal frustrations or how you enjoyed a book you just read.

☑ *Create an exciting curriculum.* Get the students involved in activities and discussions instead of passively listening and responding. This requires a lot of preparation and planning, but it can reduce disruptions.

Correcting Misbehavior

Occasionally, you will need to correct a misbehaving student. Here are some strategies to consider:

☑ *Look for simple solutions.* Make a list of specific inappropriate behaviors, then look for solutions. For example, if 2 students continue to talk, separate their desks. If students come late to class, use a stopwatch and deduct the time from their next break. Sometimes, students are able to brainstorm solutions to particular problems during class meetings.

☑ *Reinforce your procedures consistently.* Be specific about your behavioral expectations and post them. Use a reward system (see the next section). Have the consequences of disruptive behavior already thought out. Decide how you will record good and bad behavior (e.g., individually, by tables, or whole class, using tallies, stars, or stickers). Explain your plan to your students and follow through the first time a student misbehaves.

☑ *Reward good behavior.* Verbally praise the specific behavior you want to reinforce. For instance, "Ruth is following directions" or "Fred cleaned up his desk and is ready to listen" is more specific than "I like the way Ruth is helping" or "Good job, Fred." Catch the students being good, especially those who misbehave most.

☑ *Write behavior contracts.* If a certain student constantly disrupts the class, write a contract with him or her that is specific and appropriate to the misbehavior. The contract should include (a) the desired behavior (e.g., raising hand before talking), (b) how often the behavior must occur (e.g., 100% of the time), (c) the reinforcer (e.g., a 10-minute break in class each day), and (d) the term of the contract (e.g., a week or less). Note that this contract should be developed *with* the student, especially the reinforcer.

☑ *Report to parents.* These reports are most effective if they are positive. Call the parents and tell them how well their child is doing or behaving in class. If after you've tried a contract with no change in student behavior, enlist parent support. Often, parents can help determine reinforcers (e.g., extra TV time, special family event) or consequences (e.g., no skateboarding, no TV).

Remember: A positive classroom environment requires consistency, modeling, and practice. It does not happen magically.

Reward Systems

There are a variety of ways you may choose to reward your students to reinforce their following of procedures. Reward systems are used initially to motivate students to try to succeed at a new behavior. The system is kept in place until mastery of the desired behavior has occurred, and then it is phased out. Edible rewards (popcorn, raisins), tangible rewards (stickers, prizes), and tokens (points, tickets) are all low-level reinforcers. Our goal in using reward systems is to develop internal motivation in our students. Vary the rewards over time. Following are some ideas:

- *The marble jar.* The class earns marbles for good behavior, and these are displayed in a jar. When the jar is filled, the class has earned a special privilege, such as a party or the chance to watch a video. Start with a small jar.
- *Secret words.* The teacher determines a positive consequence for the class and a secret word to be spelled. When the class earns a letter for good behavior, it is put on the bulletin board. When the word is spelled, the class receives the consequence (e.g., popcorn, free play, video, picnic, party).
- *Grab bags.* Individuals earn points through academic work or behavior. A certain number of points lets them pick an object or certificate (e.g., the chance to be a team leader or special monitor, extra free time, a free homework pass).
- *Rent classroom valuables.* Through appropriate behavior, students can rent classroom objects, such as puzzles, games, special books, or toys, for overnight or weekend use.
- *Raffle or auction.* Students earn raffle tickets for appropriate behavior. After a period of time, students bring objects from home, with their parents' permission, and hold a raffle.
- *Preferred activity time.* Give the whole class unconditional time for academically related games (15-20 minutes for Around the World, Jeopardy, Spelling or Math Baseball, or the like). The time can be taken away from the whole class for misbehavior or from individuals who don't finish work or constantly disrupt.

DAILY ONGOING ACTIVITIES

Silent Reading

Set clear procedures for silent reading (for K-1, this should be called *quiet reading,* and students should be allowed to share and converse quietly about their books). Have students choose the books they will read before going to recess or lunch, and have them waiting on their desks when they come in, or have boxes of books at each table. If a student chooses short, simple books, have 2 or 3 on the desk so he or she won't have to get up. In lower grades, start silent reading in short intervals, increasing the time each day to 20 to 30 minutes.

During the first few weeks, use this opportunity to assess students. Walk around and note names of books and page numbers each day to see if students are moving through their books. Ask students to read quietly to you from their books and ask some simple questions to determine their levels of understanding. Don't verbalize any judgments to them about books being too hard or too easy. During silent reading, they may read whatever they want. Use the information you gather to suggest books that they may enjoy at the library or at other times in class. Work toward being able to sit down and read a book yourself during silent reading time. This makes a strong statement to students.

Sample Procedure Chart for Silent Reading

1. Have your books ready.
2. Come in silently and get your book.
3. Remain in your seat.
4. Read silently.
5. Read the entire time.
6. When silent reading is over, you may share something you enjoyed.

---

1. Tengan sus libros listos.
2. Entren calladitos y tomen sus libros.
3. Manténganse en sus asientos.
4. Lean en silencio.
5. Lean el tiempo completo.
6. Cuando se termine la lectura personal pueden compartir algo que les gustó.

Read-Alouds

Daily exposure to quality literature increases the desire to read independently and models many reading skills. Schedule 10 to 15 minutes for primary grades and 20 to 30 minutes for older students. In bilingual classes, don't be afraid to read stories in students' second language; think in terms of emerging comprehension. Give visual cues and use strategies such as alternate day and preview-review. (See the section on ELL strategies given earlier).

Sometimes, discuss the story with the class; predict action, clarify vocabulary in context, analyze the plot, and visualize the setting. Don't overdo the discussion—remember that your main purpose is for them to enjoy the author's work. Don't analyze every story.

Preview the book before beginning with the class. Look for appropriateness to grade level (length of passages, vocabulary, interest), and familiarize yourself with characters and points to be highlighted.

When creating procedures for read-aloud time, think about the following questions:

- Where will the students sit?
- May they draw or write, or do you want them looking at you?
- May they get up and sharpen pencils, get a drink of water, or the like?

The following chart of sample procedures assumes that you will allow the children to draw while they listen to you read.

Sample Procedure Chart for Read-Aloud

1. Get all materials for drawing before reading begins.
2. Stay seated.
3. Listen silently.
4. Clean up.

---

1. Agara todo el material de dibujar antes de que comienza la maestra a leer.
2. Manténte sentado.
3. Escucha en silencio.
4. Recoge todo.

Journals

Journals may be created by stapling several sheets of paper into a construction paper folder. For beginning writers, a large drawing space with a few lines underneath is great. By third or fourth grade, the drawing space can be eliminated. Journals are places for students to write their thoughts on a daily basis, with content being important, not mechanics. Creative spelling should be encouraged by not spelling for students. Journals may be interactive; that is, the teacher may write back to the students.

Journal writing, like any activity, must be modeled. A teacher can do this by writing right alongside students. Reading from personal journals, as well as reading from journals of historians, writers, and others, are good models for students. You can also demonstrate the process on an overhead projector to show that journal writing is just writing down thoughts.

Sample Procedure Chart for Journals

1. Write for 10 minutes silently.
2. Write about anything you like or choose a topic from the board.
3. Don't worry about punctuation.
4. Invent your own spelling.
5. Stay in your seat.

---

1. Escribe en silencio por 10 minutos.
2. Escribe de cualquiera cosa o escoge un tema del pizarrón.
3. No te preocupes por la puntuación.
4. Inventa como deletrear las palabras.
5. Quédate en tu asiento.

Figure 3.5. Calendar Ideas

Literature Logs

Literature logs are similar to journals, but rather than writing on a particular topic, students respond to literature. They may respond to the read-aloud or to their own silent reading. Their logs may reflect class discussions or just their own private reactions.

Calendar, K-2

The purpose of doing a calendar routine is to provide real-life math experiences for your students. It usually requires 10 to 20 minutes per day. As students learn the procedures, provide for some rotation so each student can be the leader. Choosing a "captain" or "helper" to help you each day allows you to become the facilitator.

Figure 3.5 illustrates various ideas for the calendar. Choose the ones you feel are appropriate to your grade level and in which you can maintain interest. Keep your calendar time simple, flexible, and interesting. As you add new items to the calendar, be sure you model them.

Setting up the calendar takes some time at the beginning of the year, but most parts will stay up all year, with just a few monthly changes needed. Specific things you will need for each part of the calendar bulletin board follow. The letters correspond to the illustrations in Figure 3.5:

A: *Month pattern grid calendar.* The month calendar grid is displayed with only the name of the month and the days of the week at the beginning of a month. The grid should contain squares of about 3 by 3 inches. Each day, add the marker that corresponds to the date. You need to make daily markers to fit the grid squares based on a pattern (e.g., shapes, seasonal cutouts, color). Keep the daily markers in the teacher supply container (see the following explanation of I). Use this to reinforce the date, the pattern, and the days of the week.

B. *Days-of-school graph.* Use adding-machine tape with a string tied through the roll so it can be pinned to the wall. Record with black each day you are in school, marking the 10s in a red pen and circling them. This graph can be used for daily rote counting activities as well as development of the understanding of the pattern of the base 10 number system.

C: *Days of the week.* Make 3-inch by 8-inch strips of tagboard with the days of the week written on them. Punch a hole in the center of each card so it can be hung from a pin and easily turned over. Turn over only those days that have already passed. This activity is done in conjunction with a days-of-the-week song (see Chapter 6). Talk about how many days have gone by in a week and how many are yet to come. Responses can be written in number sentence form (e.g., 3 + 4 = 7).

D: *Number line straw box.* Use 3 half-gallon milk cartons cut down to 4 inches high. Cover these with Con-Tact paper (in 3 different colors, if you want to make the place value more visual). Label the boxes "ones," "tens," and "hundreds." Attach a set of flip numerals to each carton. The straw count will match the days of school graph. Add 1 straw each day, bundling the tens as they occur. Use this to count by tens and ones with your students.

E: *Monthly tally.* Use a 9-inch by 12-inch piece of newsprint or a small chalkboard nailed to your bulletin board. Make a tally mark for each day of the month, circling the tens. The tally count corresponds to the monthly calendar. Count the tally marks each day, using the tens or fives as a starting point. Ask prediction questions, such as "How many more days until we can circle a 10 again? A group of 5?"

F: *Weather graph.* Make a grid with pictures for sunny, cloudy, rainy, and so on on the left side and at least 15 squares across. Each day, have the captain or leader determine the weather outside and color a square next to the appropriate type of weather. At the end of the month, a total tally can be made. Display the graphs of each month and use them for an analysis of how the weather changes over the year.

G: *Birthday graph.* Before the beginning of school, prepare a birthday cake or similar representation for each month of the school year. If you use a birthday cake, have each student write (or you write) his or her birthday on a candle. After discussing the birthday graph, use the 12 cakes and candles for a permanent bulletin board display. Put the "cake of the month" on the calendar bulletin board, with the appropriate students' candles, and use yarn or roving to indicate where each birthday falls on the monthly calendar.

H: *Date or menu strips.* Use sentence strip tagboard to make the sentences shown in Figure 3.5. Make day-of-the-week cards to fit the blanks, as well as month and numeral cards to fit the blank spaces. Also, make cards for the main-dish items on your school menu. The captain can find these cards, read the menu, and select the appropriate card, then read the completed sentences or choose someone to read the sentences when the cards have been placed.

I: *Teacher supplies.* Use a Ziploc bag or small box stapled to the bulletin board to store the supplies you will need to do the calendar: black and red wide felt-tip pens, the date markers for the monthly calendar, the day-of-the-week cards for the date strips, extra pins, and so on.

4

The First Two Weeks of School . . .
A Detailed Account

The descriptions of the first 2 weeks of school presented in this chapter are meant to give you formats that can be followed on successive days. Remember, these activities are designed to help you (a) get to know your students, (b) create positive attitudes in the class, and (c) train students in routines and procedures.

CHAPTER CONTENTS

OVERVIEW OF THE FIRST TWO WEEKS OF SCHOOL FOR KINDERGARTEN AND FIRST GRADE

Your goal for the first day and first weeks will be to build a community where learning takes place and where all (parents, children, teachers) feel valued, respected, and safe. This is a big responsibility, and the task begins the first minute of the first day of school.

Your first day as a kindergarten or first-grade teacher can be challenging. Kindergarten students may be very unsure of themselves. First graders might have to experience a longer day plus other new and unfamiliar school routines. Parents often accompany young children on the first day. Handling both the child's insecurities and their parents' concerns can be a daunting task. On the first day, you may invite parents to attend for a specific period of time. Gently but firmly adhere to this rule. Be sure to acknowledge parents' interest in their children's education; also, communicate that their participation will be valued and needed. But on the first day, you need time to bond with your students without their parents.

Remember that you will be teaching routines, procedures, and dynamics of *your* ideal environment. Also remember that on the first day, and in the first weeks, your students should be aware of and identify with *your* vision in order to become valued members of the learning community. Careful planning will see you through. This section contains detailed sample schedules and lesson plans. Here are some tips:

- On the first day, set up tables with easy puzzles and games, paper and crayons, books, and so on. (Don't include activities requiring major cleanup—your students have not yet mastered those tasks.)
- Greet children and parents at the door. Start learning names immediately.
- Remind parents that at your signal (bell, chime, etc.), they should help their children clean up and proceed to the group meeting area.
- Ask children to store backpacks, sweaters, and so forth in any available cubby. Creating names for their cubbies will follow later as a small-group activity.
- In kindergarten, arrange to have your coteacher work with you all day, if possible. Reciprocate during her or his session.

- ☑ On the first day, try to schedule aide or helper time during the beginning and end of day, at a minimum. In kindergarten, having another adult assist you all day is optimal.
- ☑ Arrange your schedule to include whole-group meetings that last *no longer* than 15 or 20 minutes. Young children tire more easily while sitting than when active. If movement activities are included, extend the time to 30 minutes.
- ☑ Be prepared with a variety of activities that focus on building your vision of a classroom community.
- ☑ Be prepared to have patience! Activities may take longer the first days.

Note: Locate at your school site or purchase one of the titles listed in the Resources section under "Literacy." To fully understand how to implement the strategies outlined in this chapter, you will need more information than is provided in this book. We are simply getting you started.

FIRST TWO WEEKS OF SCHOOL—KINDERGARTEN

Day 1

20-30 Minutes: Welcome Parents and Children

Preparation:

- ☑ Have name tags ready on a table.
- ☑ Have other tables or areas set up in the room with simple activities (e.g., simple puzzles, Play-Doh, books, paper and crayons, etc.).
- ☑ Your class list should include names, addresses, bus routes and stops, and so on—*all* information you have gathered.

Greet parents and children as they arrive. Using your class list, ask parents to review their child's pertinent information. Make required changes immediately. Ask parents to locate their child's name tag on the table and then engage in an activity with their child at another table. If possible, have an adult (aide, coteacher) supervise the tables, keeping both parents and children busy.

Hint: Prepare STOP signs to hang in front of any activity that is not open—a visual reminder to both parents and children of your off-limits areas.

After 20 to 30 minutes, make your Freeze-and-Listen signal. Model how you wish children and parents to respond. Be sure other adults respond as well. This may take time—even with the help and cooperation of all adults—to accomplish this transition. Do not give up! Practice until all students have stopped and are looking at you. *Praise, praise, praise* those who are frozen. Say something such as, *It's time to clean up and come to the meet-*

ing area. Everyone, please help to clean up your area. Parents, please help the children clean up; come and sit at our meeting area, then you may leave. We'll see you at the end of the day. You might sing a clean-up song to signal the start of clean-up.

Note: Expect some students to cry and be upset when parents are asked to leave. Try not to get upset—your demeanor and body language should convey to the child (and parents) that the child will be fine. When trying to conduct your normal routine, it can be disconcerting to have a child wailing in the background, but do proceed! Ask other adults to help console the crying child or children. Try these strategies:

- Gently pry him or her from the parent's grasp; move child to Circle Area with the other students.
- Assure parents that the child will be fine and the situation will improve if they leave. Have them leave!
- Ask another adult to sit with the child at the circle and to gently and quietly console the child. If the child is wailing loudly, have adult and child move outside the circle. When crying has lessened to a tolerable noise level, have the adult bring the child back to the circle.
- Have the child work with his or her small group. Always use words that mean *exactly* what is happening and what to expect but also ensure that he or she *will* become part of your class routine.
- For the first day, move the child through class routines. Hopefully, another adult will assist you. Instruct that person to try to engage the child in whatever activity he or she should be doing at the time. Instruct the adult to move away when the child has become integrated.
- Follow these guidelines if crying recurs. If the child is removed from class, you will be in jeopardy. Invite an older sibling to assist by conveying the message, "If you cry, you will be segregated from class routines." Your goal is to integrate the child into the class and to demonstrate that the classroom is a safe and fun place.
- Inconsolable, long-term criers (continuing for more than 1 week) might need special intervention. Parents should be contacted and a conference arranged for all to strategize. You might also contact your principal, resource teachers, or special education personnel to help devise a plan.

20 minutes: Whole-Group Opening

Preparation:

- Have available a list of fingerplays and songs to sing. Write these down—you will be surprised how quickly you can forget!
- Have on hand several simple books to read. *Spot* and *Clifford* are good choices.
- Use a puppet for introductions

Once most of the children have your attention, start a fingerplay. *Do it,* without trying to *teach it* (see Chapter 6). Sing and chant until all have arrived at the meeting area. Say good-bye to parents; thank them for attending. Reassure children that they will see their parents soon.

Introductions:

- ☑ Introduce all adults in the room. While saying the person's name, write it on chalkboard or chart paper, slowly repeating the name as you write it. Teach students to say, "Hello, Mrs. Smith."
- ☑ Introduce your puppet. (Choose a name starting with a letter not represented by your students' names.) Announce that "Beto" is everyone's friend and wants to learn each student's name. Walk up to each child in turn, saying: *Hi, I'm Beto. What's your name?* When the child responds, say: *Hello, Sandi* (for the puppet). Whenever a child is too shy or nervous to respond, simply say, *Hello, José,* and proceed to the next student.
- ☑ Sing another song.
- ☑ Follow with a bathroom tour—usually necessary by this time. For this task, another adult's help will be needed. Dismiss students individually to line up—girls first, then boys. Discuss how they should stand, one behind the other, hands by sides. Praise those who comply by stating exactly what they are doing correctly: María *has her hands by her sides and is standing right behind Jessica.*

During the bathroom tour, introduce and reinforce these points:

- ☑ How to use toilet paper
- ☑ How to flush
- ☑ How to wash hands
- ☑ Where to throw trash

Allow those who need to use the bathroom to do so. Return to class. If one group returns early, the adult in charge can start reading any available book.

60 Minutes: Small-Group Directed Activities

An appropriate focus of the first week's small-group activities is to introduce and train students to work with all materials, games, and center areas of your classroom. (See Chapter 2, "Creating the Environment," for suggestions on setting up your room.) Kindergarten provides a time block for students to freely explore their environment and make self-selected choices. For them to make good choices and work independently, they must learn the "dos and don'ts" for each activity.

   Remember: Never assume that they will understand or use materials appropriately without an introduction. Remember this each time you introduce something new to the environment!

Preparation:

- ☑ Prepare a list of all areas, centers, and activities already set up.

☑ Consider what students must know before using the materials, cleaning up appropriately, and working together at the center.

☑ Plan, in order, which centers will be introduced first, second, and third.

Divide class into as many groups as there are adults to supervise. (See Chapter 2 for color-coding name tags so you can create initial student groups). The optimal number is 3 adults. Plan to do 3 rotations of 20 minutes each for each of the first 3 or 4 days, depending on the number of activities you will introduce. The sample plan shown in Table 4.1 uses 3 adults.

Each adult oversees one activity and introduces the following information to each successive group:

☑ Purpose of the center: "At the Listening Center, we will listen to stories, using earphones."

☑ The number of children who may be at the center and what they should do in order to be there: "There are just enough places for 4 people to use the earphones at the Listening Center." Some centers are easily defined by the number of seats; others may need "entry tickets," such as clip-ons, tags, or necklaces to clearly identify who is permitted at any given time.

☑ How materials and equipment will be used: Be sure to model these instructions. For example, demonstrate how to insert a cassette into a tape recorder, then ask 1 or 2 children to model doing it. Have student volunteers model also.

☑ Behavior that isn't permitted: Demonstrate a negative behavior, such as randomly pushing the buttons on the tape recorder. Ask children to explain why it is *not* OK to do that.

This introduction should take 7 to 10 minutes, then students can work at the center(s).

Remember: Don't introduce 10 students to the Listening Center when only 4 can participate. Instead, introduce the Center together with the Blocks Area, where 6 children can participate.

After 15 to18 minutes, make your Freeze-and-Listen signal. Teachers at each center supervise cleanup, then line up their students. At your signal, groups rotate. A rotation schedule of 20-minute groups should be used only during the first few days.

Once routines and procedures are established for these ongoing activities, small-group time can develop into direct instruction. Plan at least 30 minutes for each group. If you decide on 2 daily rotations, small-group time extends to 60 minutes. We suggest a 45-minute group without rotations. After small-group time, students gather at your meeting area to prepare for outdoor play.

Remember:

☑ Reinforce what students have learned during small-group time about rules and procedures for the playground area.

TABLE 4.1
Small-Group Directed Activities

	Group 1	Group 2	Group 3
Day 1, rotation 1	Play-Doh Small playhouse Farm	Writing center	Playground toys and structure (done outside)
Day 1, rotation 2	Playground toys and structure (done outside)	Play Doh Small playhouse Farm	Writing center
Day 1, rotation 3	Writing center	Playground toys and structure (done outside)	Play-Doh Small playhouse Farm
Day 2, rotation 1	Toy shelf	Dramatic play Lego	Blocks
Day 2, rotation 2	Blocks	Toy shelf	Dramatic play Lego
Day 2, rotation 3	Dramatic play Lego	Blocks	Toy shelf
Day 3, rotation 1	Listening center Sand table	Math manipulatives	Art center: easels and watercolors
Day 3, rotation 2	Art center: easels and watercolors	Listening center Sand table	Math manipulatives
Day 3, rotation 3	Math manipulatives	Art center: easels and watercolors	Listening center Sand table

◪ Snack time may be included during this time period. Introduce and model procedures for eating areas: how to dispose of trash, where lunch boxes should be left, and so on.

◪ Introduce your signal designating the end of recess. Model how and where students should line up, and so on.

15-20 Minutes: Outdoor Play and Snack

In kindergarten, it's usual for cooperating teachers to trade supervision of outdoor play, so others have time for breaks and to set up future activities. Try to make this happen.

15 Minutes: Whole-Group Circle

Use fingerplays to settle your students. Repetition of those done earlier is a good idea. Use the calendar routine (see Chapter 3, "Daily Routines and Procedures"). On the first day, you may model this activity rather than using a student helper.

Read a story. Continue on, and you will understand why this is not as simple as it sounds! Reading aloud should occur at least 3 times a day and should be an enjoyable community-building experience. Use 2 types of reading-aloud material: (a) small-format books and (b) large books, charts, or other enlarged text.

- ☑ Small-format books—stories, magazines, and picture books—provide shared reading experiences showing why and how we read. Books chosen to enhance themes, learn new ideas, and share classic tales challenge students to be good listeners and to understand story structure and expository texts.
- ☑ Enlarged print in big books, charts, and so on, aids in teaching students how to read. Choose resource books from those listed in the Resource section. These will guide you in becoming a strategic reading teacher during shared-reading experiences.

Introduce *your* routine for reading aloud: Should students sit in front of you? Can they lie down? Be sure that all can see the book and become part of the group experience. Explain the procedure, model it, then have 1 or 2 volunteers do the same. Last, have students demonstrate that they know the procedure by inviting them to follow it. Praise specifically. Redirect those who should try again by being clear, consistent, and firm. Do not proceed until all have shown that they understand the procedure.

Preparation for a read-aloud session:

- ☑ Choose a book that will interest your students.
- ☑ Read the book in advance; consider how you can make the story come alive by using different voices for each character, pointing out something in the illustrations, encouraging children to join in on the repetitive parts.
- ☑ Plan teaching points and questions to be asked. Note ideas and questions on Post-it notes; place these in the book as reminders.

20 Minutes: Tour the School

Take a school tour. Again, it's best to divide students into 2 or more groups to facilitate learning to walk in line and to go in and out of places easily. If another adult is available, plan 2 different routes so each group will tour independently. Tours should include the office, library, cafeteria, large playground, and bathrooms outside the kindergarten room—all places unique to your school. Alert appropriate personnel to the approximate time of your tour; ask that they be prepared to briefly introduce themselves and their jobs.

20 Minutes: Closing

You've almost made it! Collect name tags. Recap the day. Students might share something they liked or learned today, an adult noting their ideas on chart paper. You might teach a good-bye song or read another story. Whatever your choice, end the day calmly and in anticipation of tomorrow's activities.

During the first weeks, remember to prepare whatever is needed to ensure your students' safe arrival home:

- ☑ Allow time to affix bus tags.
- ☑ Know which students have older siblings who will collect them.
- ☑ Arrive at the bus-loading zone with ample time to spare.

☑ Keep your class list of student information with you at all times.

☑ Arrange a "waiting spot" for parents who will pick up their children.

What's Next?

One key to a smoothly running classroom is that children *know* what to expect. After the first day, your challenge will be to establish schedules with clear routines for each time block. This might be accomplished the first day, but remember, children must practice and internalize these routines over time.

During the first 2 weeks, continue to reinforce all procedures and routines. Be explicit as to *why* routine is important:

> We need to sit and listen so we can enjoy the story. Juan, come and show us how to get ready to listen to this story. Great! Did everyone see how Juan stood up and walked to our story place? Then he sat down and looked at the book. Raise your hand if you think you can do that, too. OK, come on!

You might need to model and review often before routines are established. The key to a successful year is based on the climate established through clear, frequent, and consistent routines. Practice with students until you are successful.

The following sample schedule will lead you through the next 2 weeks. Base your schedule on when help is available, the playground schedule—any details unique to your school.

Sample Kindergarten Schedule

30 minutes:	Opening Circle
45 to 60 minutes:	Small-Group Instruction
15 to 20 minutes:	Snack/Recess
20 minutes:	Circle Time/English Language Development
50 minutes:	Exploration Time (pull a small group for targeted instruction)
20 minutes:	Closing Circle

Established Routines for Opening Circle
(these can be done in any order)

Choosing a Helper for the Day:

☑ Write each student's name on a 3-by-5 card. Hole punch 1 corner, place cards in alphabetical order on a ring.

☑ Using the first child as your helper, flip to the next name on the following day, and so forth.

Bonus: Students learn alphabetical order easily when following this method.

☑ When this method is first introduced, show students that all names are included in the pack. Assure them that they all will get a turn.

☑ Tasks for Helper of the Day: Lead calendar routine (see Monthly Calendar Lesson in chapter 5), take roll sheet to the office, serve as line leader, excuse students to line up, and so on. (This system eliminates the need for a jobs chart.)

Taking roll:

☑ Prepare a pocket chart, placing a "Yes/Sí" and "No" card in the top pocket.
☑ Write each child's name on a tagboard strip.
☑ Daily, hold up each student's name card. Encourage the class to read that name with you.
☑ As you read, use your finger for tracking beneath the letters.
☑ Following that, ask student to come forward and get her or his card, placing it under "Yes/Sí" to indicate that she or he is present. For those absent, the Helper places the card under "No".
☑ Optional: Count how many children are present or absent.
☑ Mark the roll sheet; send it to the office with the Helper and a friend. (Have an adult accompany them the first few times to make sure they know the route.)
☑ Later, you can enliven this routine: Pose a yes-or-no question. Have students use their roll card to answer on the pocket chart: *Do you have a brother?* or *Do you like to play soccer?* Students may also create a simple bar graph in response to choices: *What group are you in?*

Calendar Routine:

☑ See Chapter 3 for a detailed explanation and Chapter 5 for sample calendar grids.

   Note: Choose only those pieces of the calendar routine that students need and can complete. Others can be added during the year.

Incorporate These Activities
During Any Circle Time

Music/Movement:

☑ Songs, poems, and chants should become a regular part of your day.
☑ Singing and chanting together is a wonderful community builder, a way to relax, focus, and reenergize.
☑ Using enlarged charts of known songs, poems, and rhymes is fundamental to the teaching of reading. (Refer to your resource book.)

Shared Writing:

☑ Daily, spend time writing before the students on chart paper. This enables them to see how writing works. As you write, vocalize words, then sounds.
☑ Writing can be used for the *Morning Message,* to record students' ideas, or to pose a question during roll call.
☑ Don't drag this out; this should not take more than 5 minutes.

TABLE 4.2
Opening Circle: The Next Four Days

	Day 2	Day 3	Day 4	Day 5
Music	Sing a Hello song Revisit songs from Day 1	Same	Teach "The Wheels on the Bus"	Same
Helper	Next name	Next name	Next name	Next name
Roll	Read names Place by Yes/ No	Same	Read names Place by how they come and go from school (e.g., icons for bus, car, walk)	Read names Each child places name card on pocket chart under the symbol for her or his group.
Calendar routine	Model with Helper	Model with Helper	Helper does alone with your support	Helper does alone with your support
Shared writing	None here	None here	Write bus safety rules (e.g., "Sit in your seat. Talk softly.")	Write before roll call, "What is your group? En qué grupo estás?"
Read aloud	After introducing discipline system, read a book about a first day at school.	Read a Clifford book. Talk about how Clifford is a friend.	Read/sing a book with "The Wheels on the Bus/Las ruedas del bus." Discuss children's experiences with buses	Read The Little Red Hen/La gallinita roja. Discuss being helpful in the classroom.
Demonstration	Introduce your discipline system. Model and role-play with children. Be liberal in your positive rewards all day and all week.	Revisit and role-play problems you have spotted in any class routine Connect to your discussion of friendship from read-aloud time.	Role-play safe conduct on a bus.	Revisit and role-play problems spotted in any class routine. Connect discussion to read aloud time (e.g., "How is this like (unlike) what the little red hen did?")

◾ During the writing, speak explicitly about how one writes: left to right, leaving spaces between words, letters and sounds, and so forth.

Reading Aloud or Shared Reading:

◾ Continue to reinforce and model the routine explained in Day 1.

Demonstrations, Discussions, Whole-Group Lessons:

◾ Model, introduce, and present any new or available activity.

TABLE 4.3
Planning Days 6 Through 9

	Day 6	*Day 7*	*Day 8*	*Day 9*
Music	Teach "The More We Get Together"			
Helper	Next name			
Roll	Same			
	See Shared Writing for prompt			
Calendar routine	Same			
Shared writing	Write: "Which character would you like to be in The Little Red Hen?"			
Read aloud	Retell The Little Red Hen with simple props			
Demonstration	Revisit procedures that are not in place; model & role-play			

☑ Show and discuss realia, photos, or topics of interest related to your theme.

☑ Conduct whole-class exploration of a math, science, or literacy concept.

Continuing What You've Begun

Take a look at Table 4.2, which graphs sample activities for the rest of the first week.

The activities listed in Table 4.2 cannot all be accomplished in 20 to 30 minutes, so plan them throughout the day. Timing should be gauged by your students' attention and interest. Pacing is very important. If students are not attending, they will not learn.

Now, it's your turn. Many of these routines are in place. Using Table 4.3, plug in the Circle Time activities you wish to teach. Check curriculum guides for literacy, math, and English language development (ELD). What are good choices for Days 7 through 9?

45 Minutes: Small-Group Instruction

Once children have been introduced and trained to use various permanent areas in your room, small-group instruction becomes more targeted. If you follow the Small-Group Directed Activities plan that was outlined in Table 4.1, you can start permanent small-group instruction on Day 4.

A detailed plan for days 4 through 9, shown in Table 4.4, is based on 3 adults for group instruction. If less are available, one student group might work at independent centers (Writing, Listening, Alphabet, or Library Centers) during small-group instructional time. If an Independent Group is planned, include these centers during training time so stu-

TABLE 4.4
Small-Group Activities: Days 4 through 9

	Days 4 Through 6	*Days 7 Through 9*
Literacy	**Cut-and-paste bus**	**Class book**
	Materials and preparation	**Materials and preparation**
	Precut 3" × 5" yellow rectangles, 1 per child 9" × 12" white construction paper, 1 per child Precut 2" black squares Crayons and pencils Scissors	A short book about school: (e.g., *Things I Like/Cosas que me gusta* by Anthony Browne; *I am Six/Tengno seis años* by Ann Morris) Chart paper and pen Duplicated sheet with "At school, I like to ____/En la escuela me gusta ____" written at the bottom; 1 per child Crayons Pencils
	Procedure	**Procedure**
	Review The Wheels on the Bus Explain that students will make their own pictures of a bus. Discuss their experiences riding on buses. Model how to draw windows, door, and faces in a window on a yellow rectangle, then paste rectangle in the center of the white paper. Model writing your name on the back of the white paper. (Note: Do not write names for students. Allow them to get their name cards from the Roll and then copy their names to the best of their abilities.) Model how to draw circles on black paper. Cut them out and paste them on the yellow rectangle as wheels. Model how to draw a road and background on the white paper. Pass out supplies to children. Pass out yellow rectangles and crayons. Pass out additional materials as needed by individuals. Have each student share with the group.	Read and discuss the book Write the sentence starter on chart paper in front of the children. Have each child share something they like to do at school. Write each idea on the chart. Read each child's idea, starting with the sentence starter. (e.g., Alicia said, "At school I like to paint." Track the print as you read. Model how to write your name, then fill in the blank on the duplicated sheet, and draw a picture. In this demonstration, include how to use materials and how to clean up. Assist students as needed. Some children will be able to write independently; some will need your help. Collect all pages and keep. Make a simple book cover titled, At School, We Like to . . . by ____. Collate all student pages. During Circle Time on Day 10, read the book to the students, have them sign their names as authors, add page numbers, and so on.
Math	**Exploration of math manipulatives**	**Take-home calendar**
	Materials and preparation	**Materials and preparation**
	Have available the tubs of the math manipulatives presented during Days 1 through 3.	Duplicate the calendar grid found in Chapter 5 (write in month, year, and dates from 11 on, before duplicating). Have ready 1 per child plus extras for teacher-modeling.
	Procedure	Staple grid onto a 12" × 18" piece of construction paper; fold in half so students can first work on the calendar portion, then the art.
	Review characteristics of each manipulative (e.g., What do you notice about ____?)	

TABLE 4.4
Continued

	Days 4 Through 6	*Days 7 Through 9*
	Review how to use each manipulative. Allow children to choose which manipulative to work with. Notice what they do with the manipulative. Ask questions of individuals regarding colors, shapes, counting, and so on to get an idea of who knows what.	Select an art activity to decorate top portion of the calendar (something simple, such as a self-portrait). Number chart Pencils **Procedure** Pass out calendars. Ask what students notice. Discuss what they know about calendars. Provide some simple information. Read month and year together. See Chapter 5 for monthly calendar procedures.
Extension	**Cubby names** **Materials and preparation** Prelabel each cubby with a student's name. Write name on a piece of masking tape. Cubbies should be labeled in ABC order. Have construction paper cut to fit inside cubby. Write students' names in large letters on paper. Any collage items (stickers, cut-outs, magazines, spangles, etc.) Glue **Procedure** Show the name of each child in group. Assess who recognizes own name and reads other's names. Show collage items. Discuss how they might be used to decorate names. Have students decorate. As each one finishes, take him or her to the prelabeled cubby; attach decorated name.	**Collage names** **Materials and preparation** Cut 4″ × 12″ pieces from a variety of colored construction paper, 1 per child. Write child's name in very large, spaced-out lettering. Beans, colored macaroni, any small 3D objects available White glue **Procedure** Show the name of each child to the group. Again, assess what they know or have learned about each other's and their own names. Introduce the materials available to decorate their names. Model how you will apply glue on one letter of their names, then they carefully put materials on that line of glue. Apply a line of glue on each child's first letter. Monitor and repeat with each additional letter.

learn to work independently. Arrange for an older student helper to supervise the Independent Group. This plan uses a 45-minute group time without rotations. Each group remains with the group teacher for that time period. Students perform different activities each day; therefore, 3 days are needed for all to proceed through each center.

Have materials needed for each activity in a tub or box at the table. The content of the activities is not as important as reinforcing and practicing what it means to work in a small group. Keep activities simple. All adults must reinforce how students should sit, listen, work together, and pass out and use supplies, such as glue, paper, and so on. Those who finish early may read from the tub of books at each table.

The following sample rotation schedule includes 3 groups: Red, Yellow, and Blue:

	Days 4 and 7	*Days 5 and 8*	*Days 6 and 9*
Literacy	Blue	Red	Yellow
Math	Yellow	Blue	Red
Extension or Independent	Red	Yellow	Blue

Following group time, make your Freeze-and-Listen signal. Have the class stop and freeze. Be clear and consistent about this expectation. Ask adults and children to clean their areas, then proceed to the whole-group meeting area.

Outdoor Play, Snack: 15-20 Minutes
Reinforce expected behavior before leaving the classroom. Remind students to use the bathroom, get a drink of water, exercise, and have fun. If *you* have a break, set up Exploration activities.

Exploration: 45-60 Minutes
Remember small-group instruction for Days 1 and 2? During Exploration, all those areas or centers you introduced can now be opened. If you are teaching alone at this time, you'll want to supervise Exploration for Days 2 through 4. Your ultimate goal will be for students to work independently, with minimal supervision, so small groups can be pulled for targeted instruction. More on this later.

Each day, the areas or centers introduced during small-group instruction will be added to Exploration choices. Monitor students' progress at working independently. Redirect and retrain problem areas during Circle Time. Once Exploration runs smoothly, small-group instruction may be added.

During this time, decide *what* and *to whom* you wish to teach and in which subject(s). We might suggest Interactive Journals (see Chapter 5 on how to introduce and conduct this strategy). Or you can pull students who need certain skills for targeted instruction at their level. Refer to your literacy resource book for ideas.

Now that the basics are in place for Exploration time, you can introduce new activities to enrich the environment. Remember to first present and model each new addition during Circle Time. Examples of new activities:

☑ Simple art projects children can do on their own
☑ New toys or games

- A new story or tape at the Listening Center
- A Big Book rereading center
- Read the room
- An observation center
- New puzzles
- A puppet center
- Alphabet stamps at the writing center

The list is endless!

End-of-the-Day Circle
Conclude Circle Time activities not yet completed. A top choice for day's end is—always—to read a story.

Dismissal
During the first 2 weeks, leave ample time for dismissal and walking to the bus-loading zone. Allow time to spare. Always carry your class list!

FIRST TWO WEEKS OF SCHOOL—FIRST GRADE

Review the section on Kindergarten—First Day. Basically, you can follow this plan through the Opening Circle. For subsequent days, you might incorporate the following in Circle times (review Chapter 5):

- Shared Writing: Morning Message
- Names Activities

During first grade, a significant time block is spent developing your student's literacy skills; therefore, the first 2-week training period will appear somewhat different than kindergarten's. Your goal will be for students to work independently in Literacy Centers while you work with reading-based flexible groups. From the start, move your instruction toward having students become independent, self-directed learners—much easier said than done. Move slowly, stay with the training as long as necessary to instill independence and self-direction in your students. A sample schedule for first grade follows. Review your school's bell schedules for lunch and recess so you can determine how the time blocks will flow for you:

30 minutes	Opening Circle
90 minutes	Literacy Centers/Teacher-directed instruction to small flexible groups
30-45 minutes	Circle: Names Activities or English Language Development
45-60 minutes	Math Instruction/Math Centers
20 minutes	Drop Everything and Read/Todo el Mundo a Leer
20 minutes	Closing Circle

Day 1

Following Opening Circle, start the process for teaching students to work independently. Your ultimate goal will be to have small groups working independently at centers. However, start with the *complete* group. Plan whole-group activities until students demonstrate that they can manage a task independently and well.

Self-Portrait: Materials and Preparation
- Paper with enough space for a picture and 3 or 4 lines to write on: 1 per child
- Crayons
- Pencils

Procedure: Whole-Group Introduction
- Prepare a self-portrait on the same type of paper your students will use, but enlarge it on the copier to size 11 × 17. Show students the enlargement.
- Explain they will be drawing a picture of themselves and that you will demonstrate what is expected.
- Draw a picture of yourself. Talk about the details of your self-portrait as you draw.
- State that you will write something about yourself you want them to know about you. Think out loud about various things you might write:

  I think I'll write about my children. I have a son and a daughter. No, I think I'll write about my new haircut. It's really short, but it feels funny. Yes, that's it. I'll write, "I have a new haircut. It's short. It feels funny because I used to have long hair."

- Model writing the message.
- Discuss expectations for how students will work on their own self-portraits. Involve them in a discussion of the appropriate way to work.
- Invite 1 volunteer to demonstrate how to obtain paper and walk to his or her seat. Have 3 or 4 students model; excuse the others to follow suit.
- Float among the class to monitor behavior; give specific praise for appropriate behavior. Your goal is to instill behavior. The self-portrait is secondary.
- Make your Freeze-and-Listen signal. Praise those complying with expected behavior.

☑ Instruct children to clean up before coming to the meeting area. Again, praise those following directions.

☑ Discuss how group time worked out. Inform students what you see they should work on. Role-play the solutions to your concerns.

You should stay with this whole-group structure for at least 3 days, but don't hesitate to remain in this mode for a week or more.

Other whole-group activities could be taken from the Kindergarten Small-Group Plan:

☑ Cubby names
☑ 3-D Names
☑ Class book: At school, I like to _____ or _____. (Keep it simple.)
☑ Monthly writing sample to be posted on the wall
☑ Simple sequencing of pictures from a story you have read
☑ Copying or correcting a Morning Message
☑ Page for any class book

The Next Step

Have the class work at 2 different activities. Divide classroom into 2 areas. Don't be concerned how desks and tables are grouped, only that there are 2 distinct areas. You will need to prepare 2 *different* activities: one to be done independently and one involving you, for example, introducing the use of a tape recorder or computer. Do not become completely involved with this group, as you will also be needed to monitor the other group. Activities for the independent group should be based on the literature selection introduced at Circle Time. Some suggestions are sequencing pictures, drawing or writing reactions to the story, creating a class-book page based on a pattern. Keep the activity simple.

Introducing the Two Centers

☑ Divide the class in half randomly. Display a list showing the 2 student groups. Be sure students know *which* group they belong to and *where* to look if they forget.

☑ Devise a method for 2 distinct work areas in your classroom, each to accommodate one half of the class.

☑ Children need to see and hear what is expected at a given center. Oral explanations are not enough. Show where materials are stored, how they should be accessed, what to do at the center, where to put completed work, and so forth.

☑ Model the activities. These should include expected behaviors for your classroom community (e.g., where supplies are kept, how to obtain them, what product is expected, what to do when finished).

☑ Use a matching icon for each activity (e.g., use a pencil graphic for the writing activity, a book graphic for the sequencing activity).

☑ Dismiss one of the groups to Area 2. Praise children for walking quietly to the area and getting to work immediately. Or if they don't, bring them back and try again with 1 or 2 children modeling for the others. Then, try the whole group again.

- Send the other group to Area 1. You will want to work closely with this group on a more teacher-directed lesson but also be able to monitor Area 2.
- After 20 to 30 minutes, make the Freeze-and-Listen signal. Monitor cleanup behaviors. Praise specifically what students are doing correctly. Do not proceed until your standards are met.
- Before students move, remind them that they already know what to do in the new center—an important step in becoming independent. Instill that it's necessary to *listen* and know how to *follow directions.*
- Direct students to move to the other area.
- Repeat your lesson for Area 1; closely monitor Area 2.
- After 20 to 30 minutes, make the Freeze-and-Listen signal. Instruct students to clean up and proceed to the meeting area.
- Discuss results of work time. Inform students on what was well done and what requires more work. For at least one week, role-play behavior you want to see the next day. Each day, plan lessons requiring more of your involvement, then monitor if the other group works well independently. Do not try 3 groups until all students can work productively and independently without direct supervision.

See the *Teacher's Guide* of the literacy program adopted in your school for ideas, especially for independent groups. Refer to your literacy resource book for other ideas. Here are some additional ideas for a 2-group rotation:

Area 1: Semi-Teacher-Directed	Area 2: Independent
Introduce equipment and materials, then allow time for practice.	Make a page for a class book
Introduce Interactive Journals (see Chapter 5).	Reconstruct a poem or song. Illustrate it.
Introduce Writing-Publishing Center.	Practice handwriting.
Read a story together. Do follow-up activity about the book.	Work on name sorts (see Chapter 5).

Circle: Names Activities

During the first month of school, Names Activities in Chapter 5 should be included daily until each student has been delegated Student of the Day. Whole-group activity should take about 20 to 25 minutes. Remainder of the period should be spent with students writing their page for Student of the Day.

OR

Circle: English Language Development (ELD)

If there are English learners in your class, they should be provided with ELD at their levels of English language proficiency. Your principal can inform you of available curriculum materials. Read "Stages of Language Acquisition" (from *Into English! Teacher's Guide for Any Level,* by Tinajero and Schifini). Research whether any of your students have had language proficiency testing. List their names and levels. ELD instruction is very similar to the activities normally done at Circle Time, but instruction should be modified so all can understand and participate.

Drop Everything and Read (DEAR)/
Todo el Mundo a Leer (TEMAL)

Children learn to read by reading. DEAR/TEMAL is a time when children should practice developing reading skills. As the year progresses, you can pull a small group for direct instruction during this time, provided it runs smoothly from the start.

Materials:

- Have a variety of books arranged for easy access. Book tubs work well in that all students do not have to go to the Library Corner to select a book.

  Note: Students usually choose books with which they are familiar. Plan to place the books you have read aloud in the DEAR/TEMAL tubs.

- Have available books at your students' reading levels. They should have access to books read with you during Guided Reading. Arrange books of similar levels together.
- Include class-made books.
- Include student-authored books.
- Include magazines, catalogues, dictionaries, and the like.

Procedure:

- Have available at least twice the number of books available as there are students.
- Decide where and how they will read. Can they lie down? Must they stay in one area of the room? Can they read to one another?
- Conduct a class discussion on the treatment of books. A metaphor that works well is to liken a book to a baby. Ask if students would step on a baby, throw a baby, write on a baby, and so on. Emphasize that books should have the same treatment.
- Select 1 or 2 students to model how to choose a book carefully, then how a book should be read.
- Conduct a brief "book talk" about each of the books available. Briefly show the cover and read the title.
- Following that, have students close their eyes and visualize a book they would like to read. Ask for volunteers to share. Now, problem-solve methods for when 2 or more students wish to read the same book at the same time. Role-play solutions.
- Role-play what to do when you have finished one book and need another.
- Role-play how to put books away at the end of DEAR/TEMAL.
- Dismiss students individually to choose their books. *Praise, praise, praise* those who are reading.

- ☑ Monitor how this proceeds. Do not allow students to become restless or noisy. Make your Freeze-and-Listen signal the minute you sense students are not sustaining interest.
- ☑ Meet together as a group and discuss the results. Revisit problem areas; compliment successes.

During the first week, repeat this procedure daily. Briefly review the steps, but each day, allow more responsibility so students can explain the activity to you. Praise, praise, and praise those who can articulate the process. By Week 2, if DEAR/TEMAL is running smoothly, start pulling students individually for assessments (see Chapter 7). If not, repeat the procedure until all are reading independently for a sustained period. Start assessments or small-group instruction *only* when this strategy is in place.

> *Note: Actual reading time should be increased each day until students can sustain their reading for 30 minutes without your intervention.*

45-60 Minutes: Math

Warm-up: Start each math lesson with a Warm-Up. This is done as a whole-class activity to quickly review known concepts. Here are some easy Warm-Ups for the first 2 weeks:

- ☑ 1-20 flashcards. Look and shout the number. Look and whisper the number
- ☑ Number Flash: Prepare a transparency with dots for the numbers 1 through 6. Cut it apart. Flash a group of dots. Children shout out how many dots they see.
- ☑ Find squares: Draw a square on the chalkboard. Instruct children to look around the room and find squares. Share. Other days, they may find rectangles, circles, and triangles.
- ☑ Use any material and start a pattern (e.g., red, red, and green). Invite children to help you make the pattern as long as necessary.
- ☑ Exercises: Decide on a movement (e.g., touch your toes). Show a numeral card. Children perform that number of matching movements. Change the exercise. Show another numeral.
- ☑ Teach a number fingerplay (see Chapter 6: Ten Elephants, Five Little Monkeys, etc.). Act it out.

Exploring manipulatives:

Most primary math programs begin with an introduction to all the math manipulatives students will encounter during the year. For the first 2 weeks, you will want to follow this:

- ☑ Prepare several tubs of the same manipulative (e.g., pattern blocks, linker cubes, geoboards, unifix cubes, etc.).
- ☑ Introduce that manipulative to the class. Discuss different things you can create with the manipulative. Model and have students model several ideas.
- ☑ Excuse students to work at tables.

☑ Monitor students at work. You may wish to make your Freeze-and-Listen signal and have students walk around the room to observe what others have created with their materials, then resume work.

Skill practice: Find in your adopted math program, or create, simple skill work sheets. Duplicate skill sheets for each student. Use these as the basis of a minilesson followed by individual student practice. Or use as assessment tools to determine what skills children bring into the classroom and what need to be taught.

Ideas for skill practice:

☑ Addition facts to 5
☑ Addition facts to 10
☑ Subtraction facts to 5
☑ Recognizing and writing numbers 1 through 100
☑ Completing simple repeating patterns

End-of-the-Day Circle

Remember to conclude Circle Time activities not already completed. Always consider reading a story as a top choice for ending the day. End of day should be calm, focused on what your students have learned, and what they can anticipate the following day.

Dismissal

For the first 2 weeks, remember to allow plenty of time for dismissal and getting to the bus-loading zone with time to spare. *Always* carry your class list!

FIRST TWO WEEKS OF SCHOOL—SECOND AND THIRD GRADES

Day 1

Getting Ready

Before students arrive at class, have your day's agenda visible for them in the same place you will display future agendas. If seating is assigned, place individual materials on each desk, whatever you feel is necessary for students' first days of school (pencils, crayons, math journals). On the board, you might write a simple letter with directions (e.g., Dear Students, find your seat and introduce yourself to your neighbors.) Include your name. This sets a precedent for where students should look in the future for reminders, activities, and so on. The goal for Day 1 is to teach procedures and beginning routines. Reinforce that goal whenever you can.

Activities for the Day

All activities that will be referred to are described in detail in Chapter 5. Also, see Chapter 3 for sample procedural charts for each learning situation; detailed procedures for centers from the K-1 section may be useful. As students arrive and take their seats, make personal contact with each one. Introduce yourself to the students and also their parents, when present.

Attention Signal

After the bell rings for instruction to start, use your Freeze-and-Listen signal (see Chapter 3, "Daily Routine and Procedures"). Start reinforcing the signal at once. Praise students who followed the directions and who stopped and looked at you. Review Freeze-and-Listen procedures; discuss each step on your chart.

Introductions: 10 minutes

Introduce yourself to the students. Tell them something about yourself. Let them know you're as anxious as they are on the first day of school. Use this time to take attendance and lunch count, read any bulletins, and review the day's agenda.

Name Scramble II: 45 minutes

Explain the Name Scramble II activity (described in Chapter 5). For older students, you might include first or last names to unscramble, using uppercase letters so there are fewer clues. Have students sit on the floor as they finish unscrambling the name. Repeat procedures for sitting on the floor and for a teacher-led lesson. Display each student's name on tagboard strips and place in the center of the circle for all to read. Ask how students would attempt to alphabetize the names. Follow their ideas until all names have been alphabetized. Reinforce your procedures! Now, sort names in other ways (e.g., number of letters, vowels, syllables, and the initial letter for boys or girls). Excuse students to return to their desks. Older students are usually more comfortable sitting at their desks. If so, use a pocket chart or masking tape for taping names to the chalkboard.

Letters: 20 minutes

Explain: "Now that we know a little about each others' names, I want to learn more about what you like and dislike. I've written a letter to you about myself, and I want you to write a letter to me about you." Pass out your letter to the students, then read it aloud. Ask for a response in writing. Tell students where to turn in completed work (see Chapter 5 for complete directions regarding Letters activity). Keep letters as a baseline assessment for writing. (See Chapter 7, "Assessments," for using this information in your teaching.)

Getting Ready for Recess: 10 minutes

Review how students should leave the classroom and also how they should come in when the bell rings. Where do they line up? Where do they have snacks? Review equipment and ball checkout procedures already in place. If time allows, try a sponge activity from Chapter 5, sing a song, or read a book.

Math Warm-Ups: 15 to 20 minutes

After recess, before students enter the classroom, meet them in line or by the door. Praise positive behavior. When necessary, remind them of how to enter the classroom. Repeat procedures for working at their desks.

Math warm-ups are a transition activity used before each math lesson and are 10-minute practice sessions of computation operations students can do independently. Teach students the procedures, then explain and model the directions. Each student needs a math journal, whether teacher made or purchased. Create a transparency or large chart of a page from their math journals. Use either graph or regular lined paper, making sure your example matches the paper in the journals. Explain how students should date entries and write problems and how much of the page should be used. These organizational skills are not only useful for math warm-ups but can be used in other instructional areas. After reviewing the directions, write 4 to 6 computation problems most of your students can perform independently. Start with easy addition and subtraction facts, as their ability levels are not yet known to you. You are teaching the procedures now, not math skills. As students write and solve problems in their math journals, walk around, checking for their understanding of your directions. Using positive praise, reinforce procedures. Review answers to the problems on the board.

Math Activity: 30-40 minutes

Graphing Activity:

Before starting, review procedures for a teacher-led lesson. Ask the students what they know about graphs. Explain that they will create a graph using some of the sorting they've done, as with their names. All graphs represent data in a pictorial sense. Start with bar graphs. Write the title of the graph on the chalkboard, "Number of Letters in Our First Names." Draw a horizontal line near the bottom of the chalkboard. Beneath that line, write numbers 1 through 10, or several more than are in the longest name in the class.

Number of Letters in Our First Names

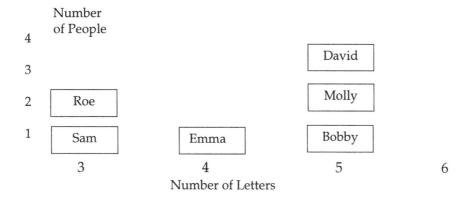

Now, have students come to the board and tape their names (remember those tagboard strips?) in the appropriate spot on the graph. Reinforce the procedures. After all have participated, ask questions about the graph: How many students have 4 letters in their names? What's the least (or most) number of letters a student has in his or her name? Most have *how many* letters in their names? Ask them to explain something about the graph. Announce that they will continue with graphs the following day. If students have been sitting for some time, try a few stretches or a "moving" activity before proceeding. If time allows, they might decorate name tags, or that activity could be saved for after lunch.

Before Lunch: 10 minutes

Review lunch procedures: Where do students eat? Special rules in the lunchroom? Review playground rules and procedures for returning to class. Use a name game from Chapter 5, sing a song, or do a sponge activity.

Read Aloud: 20 minutes

Choose a book to read aloud. Explain read-aloud procedures as discussed in Chapter 3.

Social Studies: 30 minutes

Do the Chapter 5 activity titled, "Know Your Classmates." Save work sheets for future Getting to Know You math graphing activities.

Jobs: 10-15 minutes

Announce the classroom jobs you have assigned. Show and explain the system used to rotate jobs. Role-play how one does each job. Review cleanup procedures. While reinforcing procedures, allow students time for room cleanup.

PE: 25-30 minutes

Explain procedures for outside behavior: where to meet, how to get there, signal for stopping, when to get drinks of water, and so on. Play a game from Chapter 5 or one you know. Explain procedures for returning to class. Reinforce procedures by using specific praise.

Closing: 15-20 minutes

If homework is given on Day 1, take time to explain your system. Is homework returned the following day or at end of week? What are your expectations regarding neatness or help in editing from parents? This is a good time to send information home about your homework policy. Use the rest of the time to discuss their first day, sing a song, or try a sponge activity from Chapter 5.

Dismissal

At the door, say something pleasant to students as they leave. Use their names and smile. You made it!

Day 2

Scheduling

The first weeks include teaching classroom rules, procedures, and daily routines. *When* daily activities are scheduled is not as important as *consistency*. The lessons that follow are based on a schedule that includes transitions and builds toward encouraging independent learning.

Opening

Create a relaxed way to start the day—a place to take care of business and check in with students, blending into Morning Message. The key is to gauge class attentiveness. Keep it short. Combined Opening and Morning Message should take no longer than 20 minutes. After giving the Freeze-and-Listen signal, have students sit on the floor. Use positive praise to reinforce good behavior. Use this time to

- ☑ Take roll and lunch count
- ☑ Ask a few students to share
- ☑ Review the daily schedule shown on the board
- ☑ Calendar (Chapter 3 has a more detailed account)
- ☑ Sing a song (see Chapter 6 for songs and fingerplays)
- ☑ Read a story or poem

All these activities plus Morning Message take more than 20 minutes. Choose what works best for your class. Keep Opening to a minimum, as your voice will be taxed the first few days, explaining and reinforcing. Also, students find it hard to sit longer than 20 minutes.

Morning Message (see Chapter 5)

Use chart paper for your message. Work the text for capitalization, punctuation, and the use of margins. Discuss how the date is written. Keep it short. Write this message: "Good morning! Today we will learn more about each other. You will be doing paired interviews. Let's think of some good interview questions." Eventually, you can expand lesson time to include reading instruction by "working the text." Here are some starting points:

- ☑ New vocabulary, plurals, contractions
- ☑ Vowel patterns
- ☑ Deliberate mistakes in spelling or punctuation
- ☑ Spaces left blank to reinforce using contextual clues
- ☑ Omitted punctuation
- ☑ Margins, paragraphing

Literacy Activity

After working through the Morning Message text, discuss how an interview is conducted: Brainstorm good questions, reinforce procedures for a teacher-led lesson. Before starting interviews, gauge the time so students will not sit longer than 20 minutes. Pair students in advance; repeat behavioral expectations and procedures for this activity (see Chapter 5 for directions on Paired Interviews). After each partner has interviewed the other individually, form a group so every student may share what they learned about their partners.

Partner Draw

This is a cooperative art activity conducted with the same partners. Explain directions (see Chapter 5). Show where art materials are stored and model procedures for proper use. This activity will be the students' first art experience requiring procedures. Address these questions: Are students allowed to talk or leave their seats? Can they make negative comments about others' or their own work? What if they need to get supplies or to ask questions? What should students do when the activity has been completed? Artwork should not be shared until they have written about their drawings during writing time.

Before Recess

Clean up art supplies. Discuss and model procedures: Is this job shared or appointed? Give positive praise for correct behavior. Dismiss students for recess when the room is clean. Setting up the proper routines is the goal of this first week of school. Allow enough time to reinforce appropriate procedures. Have students sit on the floor while you read a story about cooperation or becoming acquainted with new people, if available. Discuss recess rules and equipment sign-out procedures. Reinforce where students should line up when the bell rings.

Writing

Continue to reinforce procedures for lining up or entering the classroom. Ask students to sit on the floor while you review teacher-led lesson procedures. Explain the writing process; discuss what they have previously learned about the process. Explain that they have already completed the prewriting step (drawing with partners) and will now begin the writing activity. Review procedures for working with partners. Ask partners to sit together and decide their format for writing about the drawing. After each pair has finished writing, have them share their story and artwork.

Math Warm-Ups

Write math warm-ups on the board; reinforce procedures.

Math

Continue the graphing unit. Remind students of yesterday's bar graph. Request ideas for recording data permanently. Quickly recreate the bar graph on butcher paper. Start using mathematical terms, such as bar graph, mode (most frequently occurring data), range (lowest to highest data), and mean (midrange). Ask the class, "What makes a good friend?" Following a short discussion, state that you will be collecting the data. Model how this is done. Create a chart of students' names. Ask each student the question; record his or her response by name. Start organizing data into a bar graph using labels and a title. Pair up students, have each pair copy the graph started on the board and complete it. Provide construction paper and markers. End math time by showing each graph.

Lunch

Clean up all materials and get ready for lunch. Review rules and procedures after the room has been organized.

Read Aloud
Reinforce procedures using praise. Read a book to the class.

Theme Activity
Introduce *Me* Pictures (see directions in Chapter 5).

Cleanup
Review procedures for room cleaning. Remind students of their jobs. You might role-play each job if there wasn't time for this yesterday.

PE
Review and reinforce procedures using positive praise. Play a class game.

Closing
Reflect on the day. Pass out and explain homework. Do a sponge activity.

Dismissal

Day 3

Opening

Morning Message

Literacy Activity
This morning block of time could, eventually, be used for reading centers. But until reading assessments have been completed, stay with whole-class lessons.

Names
The following activities focus on phonics and phonemic awareness, using the names of your students. Daily, select 1-5 names to work with, depending on your class's interest level and maturity. As students become acquainted with this routine, you might complete more than 1 or 2 names per day. When students start rolling around on the floor, *stop,* and have them stretch. The 5 names chosen will be your first words on the Word Wall.

Name Cheer: Ask each child to lead the class in a cheer for his or her name, saying (for example) "Give me an E, give me an M, give me an M, give me an A." Chant the letters in the name. Finish by shouting the child's name.

Letter Sort: Using students' names written on sentence strips, point to one of the letters in a name. Ask all students who have that letter at the beginning (end, middle, etc.) of their names to stand up. Decide if letters in the 5 chosen names have the usual sound for that letter.

Beginning Sounds: Use first and last names for this activity. Sort names according to the beginning letters up to the vowel. Point out how the same letter can have different sounds.

Clap the Syllables: Clap the syllables for each of the 5 names. Ask other students to stand up if their names have the same number of syllables.

Rhyming Words: Think of words that might rhyme with the student's name. Model rhymes for the class; have them join in.

Vowel Poster: Construct a poster showing all vowels, including "y." Sort names according to each vowel in that name. For example, "Emma" would be in both the "e" and "a" list. Discuss each vowel sound. Underline each vowel that has a sound; cross out all silent vowels.

Write the Names: Using half sheets of paper, ask students to write each person's name. Concentrate on proper letter formation.

Have the students create an acrostic poem by writing their names, 1 letter per line, going down the left side of the paper. Say, "Think of a word that describes you, beginning with that letter of your name."

Or you might read a book about names, friendship, and so on.

Recess

Review procedures for leaving the classroom.

Writing

Start your Journal routine (see Chapter 5). Explain journal writing. Brainstorm ideas for a journal. Explain journal time procedures. Consider individual brainstorming of interesting topics for the first entry. Have interested students share ideas or what they wrote. Ask them to recall yesterday's class graph on what makes a good friend. Request a story about a friend or a special time spent with a friend. Share. Collect journals to read and respond to. Reading and analyzing what students wrote can be used as mini-lessons for class or individual students.

Math Warm-Ups

Math

Refer back to the 2 class graphs; have students think of other questions that could be graphed. Brainstorm other graphing possibilities; record them on the board. Pair students up with new partners and have them choose either a class question or one they've decided on for collecting data and graphing. Partners collect data by asking classmates the question. Give each pair a class list to keep track of their work. Have construction paper and markers available for the pairs to create graphs. To complete the process, another math session will be needed. Review your graph criteria for title, labels, correct spelling, easy reading, and so on.

Lunch

Read Aloud

Social Studies
Do Shields activity described in Chapter 5.

Cleanup
Review procedures.

PE
Choose an activity from Chapter 5.

Closing

Homework Assignments

Dismissal

Day 4

Continue to reinforce routines and procedures. Use positive praise whenever possible.

Opening

Morning Message

Literacy Activity
Before starting, review and reinforce the Names activity, choosing 1-5 new names. Ask students to complete the Reading Self-Assessment (found in Chapter 7) followed by Find Someone Who, from Chapter 5.

Recess

Have students place journals on their desks *before* leaving for recess.

Writing
Continue the daily routine of Journals. Remind students of the procedures; request ideas for suggested topics. Gather students together to explain Wiggly Line (see Chapter 5 for complete directions).

Math Warm-Ups

Math
Continue graphing unit, allowing pairs more time to create their graphs.

Lunch

Read Aloud

Social Studies
If necessary, allow students time to complete yesterday's shields. Have them pair up and share their shields. Display shields on a bulletin board. If time permits, play Bingo, shown in Chapter 5.

Cleanup

PE

Closing

Homework Assignments

Dismissal

Day 5

Opening

Morning Message

Sustained Silent Reading (SSR)
Teach and model procedures for silent reading. Allow a few students at a time to choose books or place book tubs around the room to avoid crowding. Begin silent reading. Start with 10 to 15 minutes, increasing to 20 to 30 minutes by midyear. Reading progress is determined by how much and how long one reads. Use this time to individually assess reading skills and, later, for ongoing reading conferences or literature circles. (See Chapter 7 for "Assessments" and also for tips on teaching students how to choose books at the appropriate reading level.)

Literacy Activity
Continue with Names activities, choosing 1-5 different names. An activity such as fingerplay, basic stretches, or learning a song is needed at this point. Review procedures for your chosen activity beforehand. Gather students together on the floor. Read from a book showing a clearly stated beginning, middle, and end. (Before proceeding, review Instruction for English Language Learners in Chapter 2.) Together with your class, review

each part of the book, including illustrations, listing their responses on chart paper. Discuss what is required for a good illustration and how one chooses a particular subject to represent the accompanying words. Also discuss how to choose the right caption for an illustration. Announce that tomorrow, they will complete a story sequence sheet.

Recess

Writing
Journals: Have students complete their self-assessment, *What I think About Writing,* found in Chapter 7. Have them store work in their portfolios to review for assessing.

Math Warm-Ups

Math
When graphs have been completed, share and display them. Pairs should choose a graph and write 5 sentences about the data. During the past few days, this project was modeled when questions were asked about class graphs. Examples: "More people have 5 letters in their names than have 3 letters." "Dinner is the favorite meal of the people in our class." "Volleyball has 3 fewer votes than baseball." Allow time for them to complete this task. Discuss each graph and what each pair has written.

Lunch

Read Aloud

Social Studies
Introduce What Makes a Good Listener? Ask students why we should listen. Most will answer, "to follow directions or listen to the teacher." True, but here are more reasons to listen: pleasure and enjoyment (music, poetry, movies, nature, jokes, hearing a book read aloud) and also safety and communications (directions to a friend's house). Record their ideas. Ask for a student volunteer. Ask students to observe closely what you do and say. Whisper to the volunteer that as you model a poor listener, he or she should continue talking. Ask that child to tell you about his or her summer vacation for a few minutes. While your volunteer speaks, demonstrate poor listening by interrupting, asking irrelevant questions, playing with objects, not providing eye contact. Thank the volunteer. Ask if students noticed your actions, and ask how the volunteer might have felt. With another volunteer, demonstrate this exercise again by using good listening techniques. Thank that volunteer. Again, ask if students noticed your actions. Record responses; save the chart for future reference. Pair up students for good listening practices. Have partners take turns talking and listening. Suggest they talk about their summers or their dream vacations. Decide on a topic all might use. Have pairs decide who talks first. Allow 2 to 3 minutes for talking; signal when it's time to switch roles. Bring the class together to discuss their feelings and observations. Explain that a good characteristic of a *friend* is to be a *good listener,* an important skill for communicating with others.

Cleanup

PE

Closing

Homework Assignments

Dismissal
Today, send notes home requesting that each student bring a special object and a favorite book to school on specified days (Significant Object lesson is scheduled for Day 9; Favorite Book lesson for Day 10).

Day 6

> *Remember to reinforce procedures!*

Opening

Morning Message

SSR

Literacy Activity
Continue Names activities by choosing 1-5 names to add to the Word Wall. Expand yesterday's lesson of story parts. Read aloud, choosing another book with a clearly defined beginning, middle, and end. Review each section orally. Have students return to their desks. Have them each fold a piece of paper into thirds, labeling the first section, "Beginning," the second section, "Middle", and the third section, "End." Then ask them to write about the parts of the book in the appropriate column. Ask them to share their work with the class; follow with a discussion of what goes into writing a good paper. Record their ideas for reference when this activity is repeated.

Recess

Journal

Writers' Workshop
Begin the workshop by reviewing the writing steps. Construct a chart showing key words or pictures (or both). Discuss how to decide on a topic and how this Writers' Workshop differs from Journal time. Students should have writing folders for their stories, individual dictionaries, and a list of commonly used words. Inform your teaching

by assessing their stories. If many students are making the same errors, do a mini-lesson before each workshop period. If 1 student makes an error, correct that through an individual writing conference, after first making sure that your class has an understanding of all procedures.

Math Warm-Ups

Math
Using class graphs from the previous lesson, ask true-false questions about the graphs. Have students show thumbs up for *true,* thumbs down for *false* answers. Have pairs join again to write 5 or more true-false questions for their graphs, then share with the class using the thumb technique. Discuss how to determine a good question.

Lunch

Read Aloud

Social Studies: "I" Messages (see directions in Chapter 5)
Pair younger students together rather than dividing them in groups of 3 or 4. First, brainstorm problems that could occur or have occurred at school for pairs to use in their skits. Teach this format:
I feel _____ (state the feeling), when you _____ (state the offending action), because _____ (state the consequence).

Cleanup

PE

Closing

Homework Assignments

Dismissal

Day 7

Opening

Morning Message

SSR

Literacy Activity

Continue adding 1-5 names, followed by activities for each name. After about 20 days, all students' names will be included on the Word Wall. Start adding high-frequency words to the Word Wall. Follow this 5-step format:

1. Each student should have paper or a word study notebook to write in the words.

2. As you say each word, students locate that word on the Word Wall. You then include each word in a sentence. After you have said the word, students should clap or snap each letter while spelling or looking at the word.

3. Ask students to write each word on paper or in their notebook. As they write the word, you write that word on chalkboard or on the overhead projector screen.

4. Repeat for each word.

5. Each week, add 5 new words. Practice new words for a few days, making sure to review previously added words.

Start adding more difficult high-frequency words or homophones. Include other patterns, such as contractions, common blends, and vowel patterns, as well as *hard* and *soft* "c" and "g" words. Continue the Story Parts activity. Read another story to the class. Rather than discussing the beginning, middle, and end, have students return to their seats to complete the written assignment about the parts. Students then share their work, reinforcing criteria developed in class yesterday.

Recess

Journal

Writers' Workshop

Math Warm-Ups

Math

Use today and tomorrow for assessment. Choose a topic. Decide on the data, then have students create individual graphs for that data. Ideas: a favorite meal or season or the number of tickets sold by some students for the school carnival. When reviewing completed graphs, check for students' understanding of organization for that data. Are labels included? Is it titled? Is the work accurate? (See Chapter 7 for Informal Assessing.)

Lunch

Read Aloud

Social Studies: Family Traditions

Discuss family traditions. Locate, then read aloud, *Family Pictures,* by Carmen Lomas Garza. Discuss the technique used for illustrating her book. Notice how entire pages are used for illustrations and the details in each drawing, including the clothing. If you cannot locate this book, describe one of your family traditions; use as many details as possible. Illustrate on the chalkboard how you might draw images of that tradition. Prepare a sample, either something you have drawn, an art print, or a magazine photograph. Have students illustrate traditions in their own families. Use an easily controlled art medium, such as markers, crayons, or colored pencils. Before starting, review the Art procedures.

Cleanup

PE

Closing

Homework Assignments

Dismissal

Day 8

Opening

Morning Message

SSR

Literacy Lesson

Continue working with words on the Word Wall. Add one to five names. If this task has been completed, review students' names. When moving into high-frequency words, review them before adding new words. Remaining time should be spent on the Family Traditions activity carried over from yesterday. Allow students time to complete their artwork, if necessary, but this day should be devoted to writing about the family tradition depicted in their drawings started yesterday. Tell or retell a story from your family. Have students describe or write about specific times their families were involved in the depicted traditions. Reinforce Writing Time procedures. Allow students time to share their art or stories (or both).

Recess

Journal

Writers' Workshop

Math Warm-Ups

Math
Use this time to continue assessing your students' understanding of graphing. Have them write 5 sentences about their graphs from yesterday. Follow that with asking them to write 5 true-false questions about their graphs. Collect and score papers; these will serve as good work samples for portfolios.

Lunch

Read Aloud

Social Studies
Review "I" Messages. State examples of conflicts students might experience. Have each turn to a partner, then say the appropriate "I" Message for that situation. Explain that people communicate with language, by talking, or nonverbally, through use of body movements and voice tone. Demonstrate the following examples of nonverbal communication: arms crossed across your chest, hands on hips, finger shaking, a hug, smile, friendly pat on the back. Following each gesture, ask students what you are trying to communicate, then show how tone of voice can change a message from positive to negative. Try "Oh, great!" with differing inflections to demonstrate excitement, or disappointment, or sarcasm. Have students reflect on the lesson: What did they learn? How would they sum it up? This can be done orally or by journal writing. Allow time for students to share.

Cleanup

PE

Closing

Homework Assignments
Remind students to bring a significant object for tomorrow's activity

Dismissal

Day 9

Opening

Morning Message

SSR

Literacy Lesson: Significant Object (see Chapter 5 for complete directions)
After an explanation of directions, allow pairs time to share, then have students write about their special or significant object. Have them share now or later in the day. Ask them to illustrate their objects. Bind stories together for a class book.

Recess

Journals

Writers' Workshop

Math Warm-Ups

Math: Start using math text

Lunch

Read Aloud

Social Studies
Continue yesterday's activity. Review "I" Messages, also verbal and nonverbal communication. Ask class to brainstorm emotions; write these on chart paper. If students cannot think of any, supply them yourself. Ask for antonyms for *happy* and *sad*. Before starting the lesson, have cards made up showing different emotions. Add to the stack any emotion words they might have thought of. Cards may be used in different ways:

- ☑ To alphabetize in pocket charts
- ☑ To illustrate each emotion and/or write about situations that could cause that emotion
- ☑ To act out, nonverbally, an emotion, for the class to guess.
- ☑ To form collages to depict that emotion, if you have access to magazines (ask students to choose an emotion, then cut or paste illustrations or photos from a magazine to illustrate it)

Cleanup

PE

Closing

Homework Assignments
Bring a favorite book for tomorrow's activity.

Dismissal

Day 10

Opening

Morning Message

SSR

Literacy Lesson: Word Wall
Continue to review high-frequency words added to the wall. Start the "Favorite Book" activity by sharing one of your favorites with the class. Read it aloud, then explain why you like the book. Ask for reasons why a person might like a particular book. Record responses on the board or chart paper. Have students write why the book they brought to school is a favorite. During SSR, make sure everyone brought a book. For those who did not, have them choose a class book to write about. Have them share their stories.

Recess

Journal

Writers' Workshop

Math Warm-Ups

Math
Continue lessons in math text

Lunch

Read Aloud

Social Studies
Continue yesterday's activity. Choose an idea from Day 9.

Cleanup

PE

Closing

Homework Assignments

Dismissal

FIRST TWO WEEKS OF SCHOOL—FOURTH TO SIXTH GRADES

Day 1

All activities referred to in this section are described in detail in Chapter 5. (Also, see Chapter 3 for sample procedural charts for each learning situation.)

Getting Ready
Before students arrive, have the day's agenda written in the same place you will use it on a daily basis. If seating is assigned, you might place individual materials on each desk, whatever students should have during their first days at school (pencils, crayons, math journals, etc.). You might also write your name on the chalkboard and provide a simple letter with directions, such as "Dear Students, Please find your seat and introduce yourself to your neighbors." This sets a precedent for where students can find directions regarding future activities. Remember, today's goal is to teach *your* procedures and beginning routines. Reinforce that whenever possible.

As students arrive and take their seats, make personal contact with each one. Introduce yourself to students and also parents, if they are present.

8:30-10:00

Attention Signal: 5 minutes
After the bell rings for instruction to begin, use your Freeze-and-Listen signal (see Chapter 3, "Daily Routine and Procedures"). Start reinforcing the signal immediately. Praise those who followed the directions and stopped to look at you. Take a few minutes to repeat the Freeze-and-Listen signal and procedure. Discuss each step on the Freeze-and-Listen chart.

Introductions: 10 minutes
Tell the students something about yourself. Explain that you're as anxious as they are on the first day of school. This is a good time to take attendance and lunch count, read any bulletins, and review the day's agenda.

Name Scramble 2: 45 minutes
Explain the Name Scramble 2 activity, found in Chapter 5. Start by asking students to write 5 interview questions for the second part of this activity. Before passing out envelopes, model the interviewing process, making sure you have eliminated those for students who are not present. Envelopes might include first or last names to unscramble. Use all upper-case letters so there are fewer clues. Allow 4 to 5 minutes to unscramble names and transition students to the interviews. Give a 2-minute warning before moving to introductions. Have students make introductions in alphabetical order by *first* name. Before starting, brainstorm a good strategy with them. If a pocket chart is available, students can come forward and place letters in the chart. Use masking tape for taping names to the chalkboard, or students could simply write names on the board as they come up for introductions. Follow the procedures for closure.

Letters: 20 minutes
Explain:

> Now that we know something about each others' names, I want to learn who *you* are. I've written you a letter about myself, and I'd like you to write me about yourselves. You can include hobbies, family information, what subjects you particularly like in school, and what you're looking forward to this year.

After passing out your letter, read it aloud. Have them write you their letters, using your letter as a model format. Record a skeleton letter format on the board for students to follow. Explain where their completed work should be turned in and what to do while others are completing their letters. (See Chapter 5 for complete directions on Letters activity. This is a great base-line assessment for writing. Chapter 7 also shows how this information can be used in teaching). Begin a portfolio for each student. Attach the rubric score to their letters (see Chapter 7, "Writing Expectations") and also, a monthly writing sample. Place these in each folder and you'll be ready for report cards, with work samples for parent conferences!

Getting Ready for Recess: 10 minutes
Review how students should leave the classroom and how they should enter when the bell rings. Where do they line up? Where do they have snacks? Review any equipment or ball checkout procedures in place. If time allows, do a sponge activity from Chapter 5, or read from a book.

Recess

10:15-12:00

Math Warm-Ups: 15 to 20 minutes
Before students come into class, meet them in line or at the door. Praise positive behavior—or remind them of the proper way to enter the room. Review procedures for working at desks.

Math warm-ups are a transition activity before each lesson—a 10-minute computation practice of operations and problem solving that students can do independently. Teach them the procedures, then explain and model the directions. Each student needs a math journal (purchased or created by the teacher). Using a page like that in their math journals, make an overhead projection image or large chart. Use either graph or regular lined paper, but the example must be on the same type of paper as the students will use. Demonstrate how to date entries and write problems and how much space should be used. These organizational skills are not only important for math warm-ups but also for other instructional areas. After reviewing directions, write 4 to 6 computation problems most of the students can perform independently. Start with easy regrouping and multiplication problems, as their ability levels are still unknown. Also, you are teaching *procedures and directions*, not *math skills* at this point. As students write and solve problems in their math journals, walk around, checking for their understanding of your directions. Review answers to the problems on the board.

Math: 40 minutes—Graphing Activity

First, review procedures for a teacher-led lesson. Explain that students will start a unit on graphs. Ask what they know about graphs. Record in the "Know" column on a chart similar to this one:

Graphs

Know	Want to Know	Learned

Then, ask what they'd like to know about graphing, and record their answers. Explain that you will record what they've learned at the end of the unit and that graphing is used to organize data, record information, and generate answers to questions. There are several types of graphs, all representing data in a pictorial sense. If possible, show examples of bar, line, circle, and picture graphs. (Consider this homework assignment: Have students cut graphs from the newspaper, then create a display showing questions about each graph.) Explain that they will start by designing a bar graph that uses their names. Post a graph similar to the following one in an easily accessed place:

How Long Are Our Names?

1	2	3	4	5	6	7	8	9	10

Ask each student to write the *number* of letters in their first name on a 3 × 3 Post-it Notes or on 3 × 3 tagboard pieces. Reinforce the procedures. Ask that students who have 1 letter in their name come forward, then 2 letters, and so on, until the bar graph has been completed. After all have participated, ask questions about the graph: *What's the least or most number of letters in a student's name? Which number occurs most often?* (This is called the *mode*). Start a vocabulary chart of graph terms; post the chart. Ask that students write 4 summary statements about the graph in their math journals; have students share some of these. Announce that graph work will resume tomorrow. If time allows, students can decorate name tags—or save that activity for after lunch.

Please/Please Don't: 30 minutes
This activity supports the development of classroom rules. (See Chapter 5 for instructions.)

Before Lunch: 10 minutes
Review lunch procedures: Where do students eat? Any special lunchroom rules? Review playground rules and procedures for returning to class. If there is time, students could decorate name tags or do a sponge activity from Chapter 5.

Lunch

12:45-2:30

Read Aloud: 20 minutes
Choose a book from the list in Chapter 9 or one of your own. Explain read-aloud procedures, as discussed in Chapter 3.

Social Studies: 30 minutes
Do the activity from Chapter 5: Know Your Classmates.

Homework: 10 minutes
Explain your homework system. Is homework returned the next day or at week's end? What do you expect in terms of neatness, editing, parental help, and so on? This is a good time to send information home about your class, including your homework policy. Explain today's homework assignment. During the first week or first month of school, provide each student with a blank calendar. Assign homework for that day and have students write the assignment in the appropriate box. Walk around and monitor. Demonstrate with an overhead projection of the calendar. Suggested homework for the first night: Have parents sign all school forms; bring in a book for SSR.

Cleanup: 10-15 minutes
Discuss the assigned classroom jobs. Demonstrate and explain the system used for rotating jobs. Role-play how to perform each job. Review cleanup procedures. Allow time for cleanup while you reinforce the procedures. (See Chapter 3 for additional cleanup procedures.)

PE: 20-30 minutes

Explain procedures for outside activities: where to meet, how to get there, the signal for stopping, when to get drinks of water, and so on. Play a game described in Chapter 5 or one that you know. Explain procedures for returning to class. Reinforce those who are following procedures by using specific praise.

Closing: 10 minutes

Reflect on the day. Ask students to respond to the following prompts, first with a partner, then by sharing with the class:

- Name 3 things you learned today.
- Name 2 things you look forward to tomorrow.
- Name 1 thing you might share with a friend or your family.

Dismissal

Standing at the door, say individual good-byes to students as they leave. Use their names and smile—you made it!

Day 2

Scheduling

The first weeks of school are about teaching your classroom's rules and procedures, also your daily routines. *When* daily activities are scheduled is not as important as being *consistent.* Lessons shown in the following schema are based on a schedule that includes transitions and encourages independent learners.

Opening: 10 minutes

This is a relaxed way to start the day—a place to do business and check in with your students—and blends into Sentence Corrections or Journals (see directions in Chapter 5). The key is to gauge your class' attentiveness—and keep it short. Combined Opening and the Transition activity should take not longer than 20 minutes.

Give the Freeze-and-Listen signal. Appreciate the class for getting quiet quickly. Review Opening procedures shown on the chart in Chapter 3. Take roll and lunch count and review the day's schedule, shown on the board.

Sentence Corrections: 30 minutes

(See directions in Chapter 5). This activity starts with a mini-lesson in writing. Analyze student errors from Day 1's writing activity. For the mini-lesson, choose 1 or 2 punctuation, capitalization, or spelling errors to focus on. Write a sentence on the board that has several errors. Work the text with students, inviting them to think aloud about correcting the errors. Here are some starting points:

- New vocabulary, plurals, contractions
- Capitalization
- Deliberate mistakes in spelling or punctuation

☑ Omitted punctuation
☑ Margins, paragraphing

Students will each need a journal for daily writing activities. Explain your procedures for Sentence Corrections; continue with the activity as described in Chapter 5. You might close by asking students to write the response to a prompt: for example, "What I know about plurals," "How I'll remember the spelling of 'their,' 'there,' and 'they're,' " or "I know when to begin a new paragraph when _____."

Literacy: 45 minutes

Introduction: Read "My Name," p. 10, from *House on Mango Street,* by Sandra Cisneros. Ask students for personal responses to the story. (Note: if copies or specific chapters are available, this can become your first literature study and also serve as a springboard to a writing project).

Instruction: Brainstorm the types of information Sandra Cisneros gave us about her name. Explain that students are to write about their names and then share within a small group.

Guided practice: Allow students time to write the "story of their names." Have them share, one at a time, in small groups.

Closure: Ask students to share something interesting they learned about their classmates.

Preparation for Recess
No one leaves until the classroom has been cleaned up! Students should follow both routine and procedures. Discuss recess rules and equipment sign-out procedures. Remind where they are to line up when the bell rings.

Recess

Math Warm-Ups: 15 minutes
Continue reinforcing these procedures.

Math: 45 minutes
Continue the graphing unit. Remind students of yesterday's bar graph. Start using mathematical terms: *bar graph, mode* (most frequently occurring data), *range* (lowest to highest data), and *mean* (midrange). Write these words on a vocabulary chart; add to the chart throughout the unit. Brainstorm with students strategies to help them remember each word's meaning. Explain that there are 3 major types of graphs. These can be designed from *opinions, facts,* or data requiring *processing* before being recorded. Share 1 to

2 examples of each; brainstorm others until you have at least 6 or 7 examples in each category. When students design their own graphs, they will choose from this list of questions. Some examples follow.

Opinions
- ◪ Did you like the new Star Wars movie?
- ◪ What career would you like?

Facts
- ◪ In what month were you born?
- ◪ How many people are there in your family?

Process
- ◪ How high is your plant today?
- ◪ If a = 1, b = 2, c = 3, and so on, how much is your first name worth?
- ◪ How much rainfall have we had each day this week?

Ask students, "What kind of graph is How Long Are Our Names?" Inform them, "Today, we will make another bar graph, and again, data will be recorded horizontally." Choose an opinion question for today's data collection. Model how data should be collected; work from a class list of student names. Ask each student the question; record the response by his or her name. Using labels and a title, start organizing data into a bar graph. Pair the students; have each pair copy the graph started on the board, then complete it. Provide rulers, markers, and white construction paper. (You might have to demonstrate use of a ruler.) When graphs are completed, fill in the chart you started. Ask students for mode, range, and mean, then record them. Have them write 5 summary statements about the graph, neatly, at bottom of the data. (See the following example.)

What Career Interests You?

Health	Karen	Rich			
Computers	Juan				
Sports					
Business					
Education					

Summary

1. _____
2. _____
3. _____
4. _____
5. _____

Please/Please Don't: 30 minutes
(For Day 2 of this activity, see directions in Chapter 5). The purpose of this activity is to introduce students to your class rules, which are based on how students wish to be treated. During this time, explain your consequence system. Include both positive and negative consequences. (See Chapter 3 for ideas.)

Examples of positive consequences:

- Group points for being at task and being ready
- Group with the most points is dismissed first for activities, and so on

Example of negative consequences, in ascending order of seriousness

1. Warning

2. Time out (with work) in class

3. Time out (with work) in another classroom or during recess

4. Call home

5. Meet with parents, develop behavior contract

Lunch Preparation
Reinforce procedures, get ready for lunch.

Lunch

Read Aloud
Read a book to the class.

Social Studies: 30 minutes
Introduce Partner Drawings. (See Chapter 5 for directions.) Also, you should explain where art materials are kept and procedures for using them. This is their first art experience in your class. Review procedures: Can students get out of their seats? Are they allowed to talk, say negative comments about others' or their own work? What if they have a question or need supplies? What should they do when the project has been completed?

Cleanup
Clean up the art supplies. Go over procedures needed for this: Do certain people have this job, or does everyone help? Remember to reinforce procedures and give positive praise.

Homework
Pass out and explain the homework. Students should record it on homework calendar.

Cleanup

Review cleanup procedures. Remind students of their jobs. Role-play each job, if time didn't allow for it yesterday.

PE
Review procedures. Play a class game.

Closing
Reflect on the day. Do a sponge activity.

Dismissal

Day 3

Opening

Journals: 15 minutes
Begin journal routine (see Chapter 5). Discuss: What is journal writing? Brainstorm what might be written in a journal. Review journal time procedures. The first entry might be individual brainstorming of interesting topics. Have interested students share their ideas or what they wrote. Ask students to recall yesterday's class graph, "What makes a good friend." Invite them to write about a friend or special time with a friend. Have them share. Respond to several journals during writing time, or respond after collecting the journals. Reading and analyzing what students write is a good source both for mini-class lessons and individual instruction.

Literacy
Read "The House on Mango Street," p. 3, from *The House on Mango Street*. Deconstruct the story by filling in a mind map on the board similar to this example:

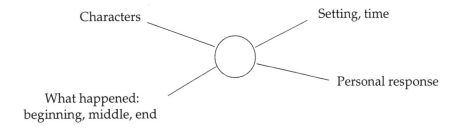

Tell students they will begin their own Memorable Moment story, starting with a mind map, then outlining the event. Those who finish early can add illustrations to their mind map.

Recess

Math Warm-Ups: 15-20 minutes

Math: 45-60 minutes
Refer back to the 2 class graphs. Inform students they will work in pairs and follow these steps for designing a bar graph:

- ◩ Decide on a question from yesterday's list.
- ◩ Predict some outcomes. Record the predictions (show students where to record them).
- ◩ Gather data on a class list.
- ◩ Organize information for placing on graph.
- ◩ Display information on graph; include title and labels.
- ◩ Interpret the graph with 3 summary statements.
- ◩ Write the mean, range, and mode beneath summary statements.

Model the Process
Pair the students; have them choose 1 class question. Have pairs collect data by asking their classmates the question. Give each pair a class list to keep track of responses. Have construction paper, rulers, and markers available for pairs to use in creating graphs. Review criteria for a good graph: a title, easy-to-read labels, correct spelling, 3 statements about the graph, and the mean, range, and mode.

Name Games, Initial Adjectives: 20 minutes
See directions in Chapter 5.

Lunch

Read Aloud

Social Studies
Do *Shields* activity described in Chapter 5.

Homework

Cleanup

PE

Closing
Continue to reinforce routines and procedures. Use positive praise whenever possible.

Dismissal

Day 4

Opening

Sentence Corrections

Literacy

Continue with the writing project, Memorable Moment. Today's reading is "Laughter," p. 17, from *The House on Mango Street*, by Sandra Cisneros. Begin by introducing it as a story about an experience with a sibling. Ask students to think about such an experience, then share with a partner. Hopefully, students have a copy of the story and can read with partners or silently. After they've read it, ask what they clearly visualized or pictured in their minds from this story. Have students read aloud any particularly descriptive phrases or passages. Discuss descriptive writing. As students develop their stories, have them focus on making pictures with their words. Pair students. Have them orally relate their stories (based on mind maps) to each other. Model this process with your story. Have students write their first draft. Announce they will get feedback and editing help from their partners before writing their final copy.

Preparation for Recess

Before students leave, have them place their SSR books on their desks. Tell them they will read silently for 20 minutes when they return.

Recess

SSR: 20 minutes

Start to teach procedures for the daily routine of silent reading (see Chapter 3 for SSR procedures). Students might record their reading and responses on a Reading Log (see example). There is a direct relationship between reading progress, how much one reads, and performance on standardized tests. One hour per day is ideal. When students can follow procedures, start Oral Reading and Comprehension Assessments, described in Chapter 7. Include results of individual assessments in student portfolios. Note tips on how students can choose a book at their reading level.

Reading Log

Date	Title and Author	Comments	Pages Read

Math Warm-Ups

Math

Introduce a Line Graph, explaining that this graph is used to chart information over time. Line graphs require some processing before recording data. Show the following example replicated on a large piece of chart paper:

Dave's TV Watching

	Monday	Tuesday	Wednesday	Thursday	Friday
5 hours					
4 hours					
3 hours					
2 hours					
1 hour					

Ask students for summary statements about this graph; record them in math journals. Turn statements into questions (as preparation for the final project). Ask students to write some conclusions in their journals based on their interpretation of the data. Explain that it is important to justify their thinking when using the numerical information they have analyzed. Share some responses. Generate a list of things they do daily that might be charted over the next week. Have students decide on what they will individually chart. Provide recording sheets; explain that for homework next Tuesday, they will be developing line graphs with their data.

Partner Surveys: 40 minutes

Do Partner Surveys, found in Chapter 5. This activity provides valuable information about your students' backgrounds, interests, and experiences that can be used to inform future curriculum planning.

Lunch

Read Aloud

Social Studies:

Give students time to complete their shields from yesterday, if necessary. Have them pair up to share their shields. Display shields on a bulletin board. If time allows, play Bingo, from Chapter 5.

Homework Assignment

Cleanup

PE

Closing

Dismissal

Day 5

Opening

Journals
See the Journal prompt idea in Literacy.

Literacy
Today's lesson focuses on *A Rice Sandwich,* p. 43. Start by asking students to recall a time when they convinced their parents to let them have something they really wanted. They might use this as a "quick write" in their journals for an introduction to the lesson. Have some students share stories with the class, or have them share with partners. Read the story aloud, in pairs, at table groups, or individually. Follow the reading by asking students if any words need clarification. Use context clues in the sentence to define them. Pose discussion questions, such as, "Why did Esperanza want to eat in the canteen?" "How did she convince her mom?" "Why did Sister Superior allow her to stay that day?" "How did Esperanza feel about the experience?" To encourage full participation, have students discuss their responses in small groups. Ask one person to summarize the story, then ask for predictions of what could happen next (as in a sequel if the story were continued). Post these words on a chart for reference: *clarifying, questioning, summarizing,* and *predicting.* Students then continue and complete first drafts of their Memorable Moment story. Be sure you have activities and procedures for those who finish early.

Recess

SSR

Math Warm-Ups

Math
Check in with students regarding their line graphs. Ask what each is going to chart; get a sampling of how they're doing thus far. Introduce a Circle Graph. Show a sample; brainstorm the distinguishing features of a circle graph. Record the ideas on a chart.

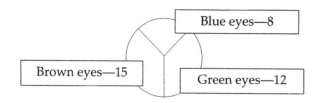

Summarize what the circle graph shows. Discuss *when* one might display data on a circle graph and *why* this graph would be used in place of a line or bar graph. Working with students, create a circle graph that follows these procedures:

- ☑ Decide on a question from the class list.
- ☑ Predict what the outcomes might be. Record the predictions.
- ☑ Gather data on a class list. (Start the process; have students finish it in pairs).
- ☑ Organize information to place on a graph.
- ☑ Display information on the graph; include title and labels.
- ☑ Have each student copy the graph, then write 5 questions about the graph.
- ☑ Students exchange graphs and answer each other's questions.

Provide students with a class list, construction paper, rulers, and markers for creating graphs. Close by discussing questions and answers.

Survey: What I Think About Math: 15 minutes

This survey will provide important information about students' attitudes toward math. (See Chapter 7 for the survey.)

Lunch

Read Aloud

Social Studies: What Makes a Good Listener?

Ask students why we should listen. Most will answer, "to follow directions or listen to the teacher." True, but here are more reasons to listen: pleasure and enjoyment (music, poetry, movies, nature, jokes, hearing a book read aloud) and also safety and communications (directions to a friend's house). Record their ideas. Ask for a student volunteer. Ask students to observe closely what you do and say. Whisper to the volunteer that as you model a poor listener, he or she should continue talking. Ask that child to tell you about his or her summer vacation, or something similar, for a few minutes. While your volunteer speaks, demonstrate poor listening by interrupting, asking irrelevant questions, playing with objects, not providing eye contact. Thank the volunteer. Ask if students noticed your actions, and ask how the volunteer might have felt. With another volunteer, demonstrate this exercise again by using good listening techniques. Thank that volunteer. Again, ask if students noticed your actions. Record responses; save the chart for future reference. Pair up students to practice good listening. Have partners take turns talking and listening. Suggest they talk about their summers or a dream vacation. Decide on a topic all might use. Have pairs decide who talks first. Allow 2 to 3 minutes for talking;

signal when it's time to switch roles. Bring the class together to discuss their feelings and observations. Explain that a good characteristic of a friend is to be a good listener, an important skill for communicating with others.

Homework

Send notes home requesting that students bring in 3 special objects for the Graffiti Board lesson the following Wednesday.

Cleanup

PE

Closing

Dismissal

Day 6

Opening

Sentence Corrections: 30-40 minutes

For today's lesson, focus on the story, "And Some More," p. 35, from *The House on Mango Street*. Start by asking what students know about using dialogue in writing. Record their answers. Give each student a copy of the story. Ask them to read it silently or with partners, or you may read it aloud. Ask what they noticed about the author's use of dialogue and why the author might *not have used* quotation marks. Using the text as an example, demonstrate where *you would use* quotation marks for dialogue. Students then use the text to fill in quotation marks. Correct at least one page together.

Literacy: 45 minutes

Model the process of providing feedback on first drafts. Explain that students will work in pairs—one reads his or her story to the partner. The Listener will listen quietly until the Author has finished. Listener then tells 2 positive things about the story and asks 1 question for clarification. Model the process with your story. Brainstorm with the class about stems that indicate positives, as well as about question stems. Record these on a chart for reference, adding to them over time.

Examples:

- ◪ I really liked the part _____.
- ◪ Your description of the _____ was _____.
- ◪ I wondered how old you were when _____.
- ◪ What did you mean when you said _____?

Partner the students, allowing 15 minutes for feedback. Monitor partners; remind them to switch after 7 minutes. Have students record the feedback at the bottom of their drafts so it can be used for revisions. Close by requesting comments, insights, and questions.

Recess

SSR

Start Oral Reading and Reading Comprehension Assessments, as described in Chapter 7, if not already begun. You might accomplish 2 assessments during a 20-minute SSR period. Students must follow SSR procedures to allow you to work with individuals.

Math Warm-Ups

Math

Start the graphing project. They will work individually on this project; explain that graphs are due on Thursday. Give students the following guidelines in writing.

- ☑ Decide on a topic for your graph. Think of a question to match your topic.
- ☑ Using the class list to record data, survey each class member.
- ☑ Decide which type of graph would best display your information: bar, line, or circle.
- ☑ Using pencil, make a rough draft of your results. Have a friend check your graph. Be sure it meets the criteria of a good graph.
- ☑ Using a ruler and thin markers, make a final copy, including title, your name, due date, labels, and pictures relating to your topic.
- ☑ Below the graph, write 5 questions relating to your graph.
- ☑ On the back of your graph, write answers to the questions.
- ☑ Attach a paragraph describing some conclusions you have drawn from your graph results. Use numeric data to justify your opinions.

Allow students time to decide on topics and questions and to start surveying classmates.

Survey: What I Think About Reading

There may be time before lunch to conduct an attitude survey on reading. Refer to Chapter 7 for the actual survey.

Lunch

Read Aloud

Social Studies

For complete instructions, see "Conflict Resolution: 'I' Messages" in Chapter 5. Explain to students that you'll teach them a way to work out problems with others. This method can be used in all situations for the rest of their lives. Share frameworks for problem-solving language:

- ☑ I didn't like it when _____ because it made me feel _____.
- ☑ I'm sorry that I (or I'm sorry that you feel) _____. Next time, _____.

A situation becomes diffused when the person with the problem feels *heard* by another. Explain that a respondent may not answer a problem with another one— she or he may not respond in this manner: "Well, I didn't like it when *you* _____ either!" Problem solvers may only work on one problem at a time. Put sentence frames on the board or a poster. Continue with Problem-Solving Skits as described in Chapter 5. Laminate both the problem-solving process and language frames on 4 × 6 cards. Place them in an envelope near the door. Explain that when students have something to work out with another, they first check with the teacher, then each takes a card before stepping outside to quietly resolve their situation. Allow a maximum time frame of 5 minutes; use only for one-on-one situations.

Problem-solving Process	*Problem-Solving Language*
Person introducing the problem:	
1. Identify the problem:	"I don't like it when _____"
2. Tell how it makes you feel:	"... because it makes me feel _____"
3. If appropriate, tell why it bothers you:	"It bothers me because _____"
Person responding:	
1. Take a moment to think about it.	Silence; thinking time
2. Use diffusing words:	"I'm sorry that I _____"
	"I'm sorry you feel _____"
3. Tell what you'll try to do next time:	"Next time, I'll try _____"

Homework

Cleanup

PE

Closing

Dismissal

Day 7

Opening

Journals
See Literacy activity for possible journal prompt.

Literacy
For this lesson, use the story, "The First Job," p. 53, in *The House on Mango Street*. Start by asking students to describe their first job. They might do a quick write about this experience during journal time, sharing with a partner or with the whole class. Have them read the story in groups of 4: Students number off, 1 to 4. Ask groups to reach consensus on how they wish to read the story: 1 person reading the whole thing aloud, taking turns reading aloud paragraph by paragraph, or everyone reading silently.

Follow the reading by asking if anyone needs to clarify a word. Write words on the board. Ask groups to choose 3 words from the list to clarify, using context clues in the sentence. In each group, the student who is Number 1 leads the word-defining process.

Next, ask the class to generate questions about the story. Record these on the board. Model the process of being a student facilitator: Choose a question for discussion and ask students to take turns responding to the question in their small groups, with Number 2s acting as the facilitators. If a group finishes before time is called, it can start on another question. Next, have the groups summarize the story, with student Number 3 leading this part of the exercise. Last, each group member is to predict a sequel to the story, with student Number 4 leading this section. Between each process, have groups share several responses with the whole class. For closure, ask groups to self-assess how they worked as a group. A survey form could be developed, with questions and a rating scale showing member participation, performance of roles, future improvements, problems to be solved by the group, and so on.

Recess

SSR

Writer's Workshop
Reading activities will soon fill the morning block; writing can be moved to the time period following SSR. Ask students, working in pairs, to peer-edit each other's first drafts before moving to final drafts. Create a peer-editing form that reminds the editor to search out the title, underline spelling errors, mark punctuation and capitalization errors, and check for correct paragraphing. Allow space for the editor to sign his or her name. Teach editing marks to be used on a consistent basis and post these on a chart. Give students individual copies to staple in their writing journals. Have students turn in rough drafts to you for editing before writing final copies.

Math Warm-Ups

Math
Begin by developing a rubric of criteria to be used for self-assessment of their graphs and your assessment of students' work. Ask them to refer to guidelines defined yesterday.

Put up a large chart to record student ideas. Ask students to describe components of a graph that would meet all guidelines. Record them in Column 3 (see example to follow).

1	2	3
		Title neatly written with thin marker. 5 questions on the bottom, clearly numbered.
		5 answers written on the back, clearly numbered.
		And so on

Have students describe a graph that would be assessed as a "1." Record descriptions in Column 1. Then, ask what a "2" would look like; record answers in Column 2. Allow students time to work on their graphs.

Lunch

Read Aloud

Social Studies
Do the Appreciation Words activity, described in Chapter 5. Follow with Graffiti Boards, using the 3 objects each student brought in on Monday.

Homework

Cleanup

PE

Closing

Dismissal

Day 8

Opening

Sentence Corrections

Literacy
Begin with a portion of core literature or a short story, using the reading process described in Day 7. Introduce the story through theme, predictions, book jacket, and so on.

Have students read to a certain point, deciding together how that section should be read. Invite class to generate words to be clarified; record them on the board. Ask Number 2 students to lead their group in defining words. Model, then check for understanding. Share definitions. Ask groups to generate questions about the selection and share them with the whole group; record them. Number 3 students are to then choose a question and facilitate the discussion in their groups. Share several discussion highlights with the whole class. Number 4 students then lead the summarization; Number 1 students lead predictions for the next section. Close by asking for personal connections with the story's theme thus far.

Recess

SSR

Writer's Workshop
Return students' papers with your edits; have them write final drafts. Provide appropriate paper, decide whether students should use pencil or pen, whether to print or write in cursive, and where illustrations should be placed. Announce that they will illustrate their stories tomorrow.

Math Warm-Ups

Math Lesson
Have students complete graph projects. Have something ready for those who finish early.

Lunch

Social Studies
Continue Chapter 5's Problem-Solving Skits, begun on Day 6. Give instructions, then explain that people communicate 75% of what is said by nonverbal actions, with our bodies or tones of voice. Demonstrate examples of nonverbal communication by using your body: a hug, smile, friendly pat on the back, arms crossed against the chest, hands on hips, the shake of a finger, and so on. Following each gesture, ask students what you are trying to communicate. Now, show how tone of voice can change a message from positive to negative. Try, "Oh, great!" with differing inflections that can mean excitement, or disappointment, or sarcasm. Invite students to integrate nonverbal language into their skits. Following skits, have students reflect on what was learned—either orally or by journal writing. Have them share.

Homework

Cleanup

PE

Closing

Dismissal

Day 9

Opening

Journals

Literacy

Continue reading the piece of literature begun yesterday, or introduce a new short story. You might start by summarizing where yesterday's story left off, with predictions for today. If working with a new piece of text, introduce the story's theme, connecting it with students' lives. Rotate roles: Today's Number 3s will lead the defining of words, Number 4s will be the facilitators, Number 1s will lead the summarizing, and Number 2s will ask for predictions. Explain that, after following today's reading (a modified version of Reciprocal Teaching), each person in each group will be responsible for recording something. Lead the class through the 4 steps: clarification of vocabulary words, discussion, summarizing, and predicting. Provide work sheets for each role; give work sheets to the appropriate students. Allow time for the Clarifiers to record sentences, with chosen words underlined and definitions generated by the group. Discussion directors are to record the discussion question and the group's responses. Summarizers record the group's summary; Predictors record the group's predictions. Allow time for sharing with the whole group; reflect on the activity and also the group process. Model the 4 recording tasks on an overhead projector screen. Before proceeding, check to see that all the students understand what they're to do.

Recess

SSR

Writer's Workshop

Students illustrate their stories. Provide a variety of art materials. Make sure students know your procedures for acquiring and using materials and cleaning up. Before they start drawing, you might use picture books to model a variety of illustrative styles.

Math Warm-Ups

Math Lesson

Return to the original KWL chart. Ask students to write what they've learned in this graphing unit. Encourage sharing and record comments on the class chart. Give students a typed copy of the rubric they developed yesterday. Have them self-assess their graph by following the rubric's criteria, underlining those elements that reflect their work. Below the rubric, leave space for students to write the score they feel they deserve and why. Leave another space for students to write a personal goal for their next math project. Have them trade their graphs with a partner. Each student should read the partner's graph and answer the 5 questions (without looking on the back!). Students return graphs to their owners, who then correct the paper. Allow time for pairs to discuss their work. Explain that you will score graphs on a separate rubric, attaching it to theirs. Post the graphs, and you're ready for Back to School Night!

Lunch

Read Aloud

Social Studies

Continue yesterday's activity. Review "I" Messages, also verbal and nonverbal communication. Have the class brainstorm emotions; write these on chart paper. Sort into a T chart according to positive and negative emotions. Discuss negative emotions as those with the capacity to trigger automatic responses before one can decide how to respond. Write the word *responsibility* on the board. Separate this word into parts; state that *responsibility* is one's ability to respond. You might then do one of the following activities:

- Write a situation that would cause someone to feel a particular emotion; have students guess that emotion.
- Have students act out emotions nonverbally for the class to guess.
- Have each student choose an emotion, then cut images from magazines to create a collage depicting that emotion.
- Ask students to create a poem, song, rap song, and so on illustrating specific emotions.

Close by discussing why it's important to identify emotions and how to develop strategies to deal with negative feelings. Brainstorm how this could enhance their lives now and in the future.

Homework

Cleanup

PE

Closing

Dismissal

Day 10

Opening

Sentence Corrections

Literacy
Continue with the same literature as before or start a new short story. Use the modified Reciprocal Teaching Process. Using the overhead projector, model how you wish the recording to be done; share positive examples from yesterday's work. Follow the recording by having students fill out the attitude survey from Chapter 7, What I Think About Writing.

Recess

SSR

Writer's Workshop
Model writing the cover, title page, and "About the Author" segments of the writing project. Use different books for modeling what should be included and how different authors perform this task. You might create an About the Author form to be pasted into the back cover. Use construction paper for covers, and if your school has a spiral-binding machine, use that for binding the books.

Next week, have students self-assess their stories using the Writing Expectations found in Chapter 7. Have them set a writing goal to refer to for the next writing assignment. After scoring the stories with the Writing Expectations rubric, share your assessments with students. Collect prewrites and first drafts, staple to the rubric scores, and place in students' portfolios. Next week, allow 15 to 20 minutes per day for Author's Chair, so students can read and share their final work. Display books for them to read during SSR. Add the completed books to portfolios for parent conferences.

Math Warm-Ups

Math
Give students a pretest covering the first chapter of the math text to be addressed. Usually, in intermediate grades, revisiting place value, rounding or estimating, greater than/less than, and regrouping are appropriate starting points. If your district uses materials other than textbooks, assess students' prior knowledge using the best available method. Assessments help develop your next unit and reveal modifications needed in your instruction.

Lunch

Read Aloud

Social Studies

Use the Group Definition of Cooperation and Cooperative Triangles activities described in Chapter 5, to reinforce cooperative behaviors. Close this unit on Getting to Know You by reflecting with your students about what they have learned.

Homework

Cleanup

PE

Closure

Dismissal

5

Activities for the First Month

Activities for the first month of school should build self-esteem, foster classroom unity, allow you and your students to get acquainted, and generate student excitement about being in your classroom.

CHAPTER CONTENTS

Appreciation Words

Materials: paper, pencils, chart paper (optional)
Grouping: whole class and teams
Approximate Time: 20-30 minutes
Directions:

1. Choose one child for demonstration purposes, and write a list of 6-10 words describing that person. Use words that describe his or her special attributes, such as *caring, helpful, a good listener, friendly, good at sports, creative, thoughtful,* and *contributes to class discussions.* Review the procedures for teacher-led discussion.

2. Have the class guess who the person might be. Write each guess on the board.

3. After several guesses, tell the class that all their guesses are right in a way, because all of the people they guessed have these characteristics.

4. Tell them the name of the person you thought of when making the list.

5. As a class or in teams, brainstorm words of appreciation. It might help if you ask the students to think about particular people. Younger students could think about characters from a book you have read to them. Make a list from the students' suggestions and display it in the room.

Extension: Throughout the year, have the class develop a list of appreciation words for a special student. Record the words on chart paper for the student to take home at the end of the week. Students may also sign the chart or write personal comments and compliments on it before it is taken home. Periodically, discuss words from the list (their meanings, the type of things a person would do to exhibit a particular attribute, and so on) and add a couple of the words to your regular spelling list.

Characteristics: Following is a list of words that might help you with this activity if the class gets stuck. You might also give students the task of alphabetizing these words.

friendly	cheerful
helpful	loyal
responsible	flexible
reliable	creative
generous	energetic
thoughtful	outgoing
caring	courageous
humorous	resourceful
polite	willing
eager	organized
enthusiastic	compassionate
fair	considerate

A list of Spanish words may also be useful:

amistoso	enérgico
agradable	interesante
compasivo	deseoso
productivo	comprensivo
generoso	selectivo
beneficioso	amable
intrépido	responsable
inventivo	habil
justo	entusiasta
considerado	alegre
cortéz	puntual
vigoroso	estudioso
inspirado	capaz
flexible	

Positive Adjectives

Materials: tagboard, tape, pencils
Grouping: whole class
Approximate Time: 45 minutes
Directions:

1. As a class, brainstorm a large list of positive adjectives.

2. Split the class up into cooperative groups or partners and have students come up with 10 positive adjectives for one another.

3. As an alternative, you can tape a piece of tagboard with lined paper attached to each person's back. Tell the students that when you give the signal, they are to see how many different people's backs they can write positive adjectives on (have them initial the adjectives). A team may sit down as soon as each person on the team has 10 adjectives.

4. Have students recopy the positive adjectives about themselves, using "I am . . ." or "John says . . ." forms (for example, "I am intelligent," or "Mary thinks I'm fascinating").

Closure: Have a discussion about how the activity made students feel. Ask, "What can we learn from this that will make our class a nicer place to be?"

Bingo

Materials: enough Bingo game sheets for all students (see following page), all students' names written on separate pieces of paper, a bag or other container to put the names in, "prizes"

Grouping: whole class

Approximate Time: 20-30 minutes

Directions:

1. Have paper monitors pass out the Bingo sheets.

2. Explain the directions and your behavioral expectations. Tell the students, "This activity is a fun way to learn your classmates' names. At the signal, write one name in each box on the Bingo sheet. Do not use any name twice. Try to write as many names as you can from memory. You may use your own name. Then, I will pull a name from this bag. If you have that name on your Bingo sheet, cross it off. When you have 5 names crossed off in a row, vertically, horizontally, or diagonally, say 'Bingo.'"

3. Check for the students' understanding of the directions, then give the signal to start.

4. Circulate around the room to prompt students. They should be able to fill in the names on their sheets in 5-10 minutes, depending on the grade level. For younger students, (a) make a game board with fewer boxes, (b) write students' names so that they just need to recognize the beginning sounds, and (c) have students work in pairs.

5. Give your zero-noise signal and repeat the procedure again if the students begin to call out during the game.

6. Play until someone says, "Bingo." Verify the names he or she has crossed out with the names you've pulled out of the bag. Continue play until another student has Bingo. Repeat until several students "win."

7. Give out prizes of graham crackers, raisins, popcorn, or the like. Be sure everyone gets a prize. You might want to give the "winners" a little more. This game is good to play right before recess, so the students can be excused as soon as they get their snacks.

BINGO

		FREE		

Monthly Calendar Lesson

The following calendar grid(s) can be used each month as a directed lesson on calendar skills and number writing. Sending a calendar home each month with an art project and poem or song that reflect your theme is an easy and effective way to communicate with parents.

Materials: calendar grids (on the following pages), construction paper

Grouping: small groups or entire class

Preparation:

- For kindergarten: Write the month and year and fill in the dates above the number 10 at the beginning of the year. Duplicate a copy for each child plus an extra for yourself.
- For First Grade: Leave all dates blank. Duplicate a copy for each child plus an extra for an overhead transparency if you plan to do the lesson with the whole class.
- Staple a copy of the calendar grid to the bottom of a 12 × 18 piece of construction paper.
- Plan and duplicate a simple art project that represents what you will be studying that month. You may also wish to duplicate a reduced version of a song or poem that the children are learning.

Procedure:

1. The first time you do the calendar, you will want to do a directed lesson. Model writing each number, then ask the children to write the number. For first grade, you may wish to model writing a series of numbers, then have children write them.

2. Model how to complete the art project before you ask children to do it independently.

Follow-up ideas:

- Send the calendar home, with instructions on using it, as part of homework. For example, prepare a simple list of questions that children can complete with their parents: How many Tuesdays are there in September? Does anyone in your family have a birthday in September? When?
- Post the calendar in your classroom. Use it to model how to write important upcoming events at school and in your classroom. Encourage children to use the calendar to count the number of days until an upcoming event, and so on.

Monday	Tuesday	Wednesday	Thursday	Friday	Saturday	Sunday

Domingo	Lunes	Martes	Miercoles	Jueves	Viernes	Sabado

Conflict Resolution: "I" Messages

Materials: none

Grouping: cooperative groups of 4

Approximate Time: 60 minutes

Directions:

1. Tell your students you'll all be working on skits in which they'll be practicing "I" messages. Give sample "I" messages, such as, "I can't think with a lot of noise."

2. Act out the following skit for the class:
   First person: Jane's hogging the ball. She won't let me play.
   Second person: You're too dumb to play. You don't even know how to play the game. You're a tattletale. (Runs off to join other friends.)

3. Talk about what happened and the kind of message it was. ("You" message, blaming, didn't tell how they felt or what they needed from the other person. No compromise happened.)

4. Ask what could have been said instead. Ask, "How can we give better 'I' messages?" Generate ideas. Have two students act out a better way to resolve the conflict.

5. Generate a list of things that make students angry. List them on the board.

6. Divide the class into groups of 4. Tell them that each group needs to create a skit in which 1 person gets angry at another. Two students from the group will act out the skit with "you" messages, and then the other 2 students will reenact the skit with "I" messages and compromise.

7. Explain procedures—where you want students to work, the acceptable noise level, and so on. Discuss how the groups might choose the characters for their skits fairly. Give the groups 10-15 minutes to work on their skits.

8. Bring the students back to their seats and have each group perform its two skits.

Closure: Ask, "What did the groups do differently in the second skits? What did you learn today about resolving conflicts? How can practicing this help our class?"

The Garfunkle Story

Materials: 1 large basic paper doll made of construction paper

Grouping: whole class

Approximate Time: 20 minutes

Directions:

1. Hold up the paper doll in front of the class and introduce him as Garfunkle. Explain a very tough day in his life: He got up late, his mother yelled at him, he spilled his breakfast, he missed his bus or got a bus citation, and on and on, using examples the kids can relate to in your school. It is particularly good to use things you've seen happen in the class. With each negative incident, fold in a little part of Garfunkle's body to make the doll shorter, and explain how he felt bad and that made him feel smaller. Keep folding in the parts as he gets smaller and smaller. Have him do something such as tease someone or hit someone to try to feel bigger, but instead he gets in trouble and feels even smaller. When you get to the end of your story, Garfunkle should be all folded up.

2. Talk with the class about how it feels at times like that. Ask how many of them have felt that way at times. Brainstorm ways that the kids in Garfunkle's class could make him feel better. Write them on the board.

3. Continue the story, using the ideas the class came up with, opening up Garfunkle with each positive experience until he is whole again. Talk about how you have Garfunkles in the class every day.

Closure: Ask, "How can this story help make our class better?"

Follow-Up: Copy the brainstormed list and post it with Garfunkle to remind students of the kinds of things they can do to help each other feel good and whole.

Group Definition of Cooperation

Materials: large pieces of paper, crayons or markers, writing paper, pencils

Grouping: cooperative groups of 3 or 4

Approximate Time: 45-60 minutes

Directions:

1. Students in cooperative groups number off 1-3 or 1-4, depending on group size. Give each number a job: recorder, reporter, timekeeper, "gopher" (the recorder writes down the group's ideas and final definition, the reporter reports the group's ideas to the class, the timekeeper keeps track of the group's 5 minutes for discussion, and the gopher gets the paper and pencils the group needs).

2. Tell students that each group will be coming up with a definition of cooperation. All group members must participate and come to consensus on the definition.

3. Give each group a large piece of paper to draw a mural that reflects the group's definition. Discuss cooperation and involvement of every student in the group. Give approximately 30 minutes for the drawing.

4. Have the reporters share their groups' definitions of cooperation and their murals.

Closure: Ask students, "How will cooperation help our class this year? What kinds of things can students do to show cooperation—what does cooperation look like and sound like?" Ask each student to tell his or her group one thing he or she liked about the way the group worked today, or have individual students write or tell one thing they liked about their own behavior and one thing they can improve.

Group Definition of Cooperation: Extensions for Younger Students

- Option 1: Start with a drawing on butcher paper. Cut into enough puzzle pieces for each student to have a piece, or glue a poster on oak tag and cut into puzzle pieces.
- Option 2: Purchase a large floor puzzle with enough pieces for everyone in the class. Have the students sit in a circle with their puzzle pieces. Review procedure for putting the pieces together.
- Option 3: Cut a large piece of butcher paper into puzzle pieces, one for each student. Have students draw something about themselves on their puzzle piece. Put this together for a perfect fit!

Follow the puzzle completion with a brief discussion on how all students cooperated in making the complete picture.

Interactive Writing: Interactive Journals

Preparation: Prepare journals for each child. Staple 20-30 sheets of writing paper into construction-paper covers—or use 3-prong report covers, if available.

Introducing Interactive Journals: Demonstrate the following process several times before your class. If possible, demonstrate with another adult (have one person play the student's role). If not, use several students.

Procedure:

1. Student writes or draws on one page of her or his journal.

2. Student "reads" journal entry to teacher.

3. Teacher responds to entry orally, engaging the child in conversation.

4. Teacher responds to the entry in written form—as a comment or question—then models writing, slowing speech to match the writing.

5. Teacher invites student to read the response.

6. Teacher mediates (scaffolds) the student's attempts to write a response.

Considerations:

☑ Interact and respond to each entry. Do not ask students to write in their journals if you cannot respond.

☑ Provide immediate response and scaffolding for emergent writers. Their writing and message will not "carry" over time.

☑ Respond to content before mechanics, or students may become reluctant risk takers.

☑ Do not provide prompts. The student's writing comes from within and should express his or her own voice. Work with a student who has difficulty finding a topic. Brainstorm or engage in conversation about her or his life and interests.

☑ Scaffolding is individualized. The key teaching points evolve from student's developmental writing stages.

☑ Journal entries provide a developmental history of a child's writing. Put copies of these entries (over time and place) into the student's portfolio. These samples communicate progress to parents and provide ideas on how their child may be helped at home.

Shared Writing

Morning Message

This is a shared writing activity. The teacher models writing while showing students the relationship between the spoken and written words. Specific mechanics or concepts about print are explicitly explained and modeled.

Keep your messages brief at the start of school year. Create messages that build your classroom community and are relevant to students' lives and experiences (e.g., In Room 2, we are learning about how to cooperate). Vary these messages: Include fact, fiction, rhymes, questions, exclamations, and letter writing.

Crucial to implementing this strategy is the metacognition a teacher demonstrates to her or his class, talking through thinking. Follow this process:

1. Appear to think about what you might write. Discuss your various ideas.

2. Write a message. Think aloud as you write; discuss each aspect of your writing (e.g., When I start to write a sentence, I must remember to use a capital letter).

3. Have students read the message as you write (include rereading from the beginning). You are now modeling the process that writers use when they recapture beginning thoughts and ideas, before completing their piece.

4. On completion of your message, guide students in rereading it fluently.

5. Work the text by asking children to identify and mark various concepts about print and mechanics. (See the following section).

6. Soon after Morning Message, students should have an opportunity to write independently, either in a Morning Message Journal or an Interactive Journal or by becoming involved in Writer's Workshop.

Working the Text

Have students circle, underline, or in some way mark these aspects of text:

- Capital letters
- Rhyming words
- Words beginning with the same letter
- Punctuation
- Spaces between words
- Words with the same sound
- Upper and lower case differences
- Little words inside big words: "mar" is inside "mariposa;" "he" is inside "she"
- Words that are the same
- Names
- Number of words in a sentence
- Number of sentences
- *Where* to start writing; *where* to proceed after getting to the end of a line

Names Activities

Names is a start-of-the year, shared-writing activity for kindergarten and First Grade, although it can be adapted for higher grades. Names teaches the names and sounds of upper and lower case letters, concepts about print (how and why letters go together to create words, sound and spelling in correspondence, and how to recognize patterns, similarities, and differences in print features).

Procedure for Names Activity: First, select one child as *student of the day*. That student's name will progress through the following steps:

1. In advance, write the chosen name on a long strip of paper—one that can be stapled to form a "crown" worn by the *student of the day*.

2. On a tagboard strip, slowly write the name while saying the letters aloud. Tape to chart paper.

3. Count the letters in the name with the whole group.

4. Repeat the name. Chant the letters while clapping on each one.

5. Discuss the capital letter.

6. Write the name on the chart paper; have students chant the spelling as you write.

7. Remove the tagboard name card from chart paper. Have students watch as you cut apart each letter. Mix up all letters in a pocket chart.

8. Invite several students to rearrange the letters to form the name.

9. Invite the class to chant the letters. Have them check to see if the name is in the correct order. Slide your finger under each letter to guide chanting.

10. Discuss the name. Focus on concepts about print (e.g., how the name begins and ends, the first or last letter, same letters, different letters, a long or short name, etc.).

11. Interview the student and write a chart story about her or him. Model and think aloud about writing and how mechanics are used when writing.

12. Work the text. (See Morning Message for ideas).

13. At writing tables, have students write or draw a picture for the student of the day.

14. Students share their writing and drawings with the group. You might decide on only 5-6 students to share each day.

15. Compile children's writing into a book. Send the book home with the student of the day.

16. Leave the name chart story on display for students to reread.

Moran, C., Stobbe, J., Baron, W., Miller, J., & Moir, E. Keys to the Classroom, Second Edition. Copyright © 2000, Corwin Press, Inc.

Journals (Grades 2-6)

Journal Prompts

Build on your students' interests, hobbies, experiences, and family background with journal prompts. Invite them to write about subjects or places they would like to explore. Weave in informational facts from their community and the world that might interest them or affect their lives:

- If you had all the time in the world, where would you travel?
- If you were a famous athlete, what sport would you play? What would your life be like?
- It's a sunny Saturday, and you and your friends _____.
- Yesterday, the local skateboard park was closed indefinitely due to a serious injury. How do you feel about that? What do you think should happen as a result?
- If you could take only 3 people with you on a trip around the world, who would you choose? Why?
- What are the qualities of a great teacher?
- What are the ingredients for a perfect summer?
- When you can't fall asleep, what do you think about?
- What is something that makes you feel happy?
- What is something that you find scary?
- What kind of animal would you like to be?
- What makes you feel frustrated?
- What makes you laugh?
- If you were lost in the woods and it got dark, what would you do?
- What do you think you might be doing in 25 years?
- What are your best qualities?

Sentence Corrections

Sentence corrections can be a daily transition activity but should be followed by mini-lessons on the mechanics of writing.

Materials: Sentence Corrections Journal or a specific tab in student binder; pencils, 2 sentences written incorrectly on the board or transparency, answer key

Grouping: individual

Approximate time: Weekly mini-lesson: 20 minutes; daily practice: 10-15 minutes

Introduction: Prior to the lesson, assess student writing to determine the kinds of errors they are making. Design a lesson for the whole class or small groups, depending on the need. Provide mini-lessons showing run-on sentences, fragments, use of capitalization, or other needed skills. Follow with daily opportunities for students to practice their skills by correcting sentences on the board.

Instructions: After students come in from recess, have them copy the 2 sentences into their journal (or binder paper), making the appropriate corrections as they write. Be clear on what they should do when work has been completed.

Guided practice: Correct the two sentences with your students. Invite a volunteer to come to the board (or overhead) and make the first revision. Always ask for an explanation of the student's thinking, such as: "What rule were you following?" or "How did you know to make that change?" If the revision is incorrect, ask, "Does anyone have another idea for this revision?" Again, ask for student thinking concerning the change. Let them know the correct answer, then ask them to make the change in their entry. Continue until all necessary changes have been made.

Closure: Ask students to write (or describe to a partner) what they learned in terms of grammar, spelling, or mechanics. Allow a few minutes for whole-group sharing. Periodically, have students write their goals for Sentence Corrections. Check back in a week or so for personal reflection and assessment of progress.

Ideas for Mini-Lessons

Instructions: Teach each of these skills within context. Model the concepts by thinking aloud during Morning Message. Also, request contributions from students.

- Using capital letters to start sentences
- Using capital letters for proper nouns
- Using periods
- Using question marks
- Using exclamation marks
- Using quotation marks
- Using possessives ('s)
- Using apostrophes with contractions
- Using plurals
- Using "ed" endings
- Using commas to separate items in a series
- Using commas in the greeting and closing of a letter
- Using colons
- Using semicolons
- Using parentheses
- Run-on sentences
- Homonyms

Problem-Solving Skits

Materials: vignettes of typical group problems (home or school) likely to happen within your students' age group; these should be on index cards (one per group) along with a chart of criteria for skits.

Grouping: groups of 3 or 4 students, selected randomly

Approximate Time: 45 minutes

Introduction: Ask students, "When you have a disagreement with friends, what do you do? How do you resolve your problems?" Solicit ideas from the group; record them on the board. You may get answers such as, "We talk about it until we agree, or we toss a coin." Accept all reasonable answers.

Instructions: Tell students they will be working within a group to solve a problem. Each group will receive a vignette, or story, that exemplifies a problem. Allow the group 10 minutes to brainstorm on solving that problem, and develop a skit to perform in class demonstrating the problem and solution. State that they will be placed in groups, randomly, and must follow several criteria. (Record these on board, chart, or overhead):

◪ Everyone must participate in the skit
◪ The skit must show both problem and solution
◪ The solution must be satisfactory to all in the group
◪ If anyone disagrees with the solution, the group must brainstorm until an agreement is reached

Guided practice: Form random groups of 3-4 students. Number them off and assign student roles of recorder, facilitator, timekeeper, and so on. Check for understanding of roles. Ask how it will look or sound when the group is working cooperatively. Allow 15 minutes for skit development. Monitor the level of cooperation within groups.

Closure: Ask each group to perform their skit. Allow several compliments from the class regarding solution and performance. Point out specific examples of cooperation within groups as they worked on skit development. Ask how students might apply what they have learned.

Possible Problem-Solving Vignettes

- ☑ It is a Saturday, and 4 friends want to get together. However, one wants to see a movie, one wants to go boogie-boarding at the beach, another wants to ride bikes, and the fourth wants to go to the mall. How will you solve this problem so all 4 friends spend the day together and are happy with their chosen activity?

- ☑ Four students are playing four-square during recess. One student calls another out. However, that student disagrees and refuses to leave the game. What do you do?

- ☑ Two friends agree to play together at recess. One person broke his or her agreement and went off to play with others during recess. How can this be resolved?

- ☑ Three students were playing at recess. A fourth asked to join in, but the others in the group wouldn't let him or her join them. What happens?

- ☑ The class is taking a math quiz, and a student notices someone copying his or her answers. What does he or she do?

Know Your Classmates

Materials: enough teacher-made work sheets for all students, pencils
Grouping: whole class
Approximate Time: 30 minutes
Directions:

1. Make your own work sheet with the blanks shown on the following 2 pages.

2. Have paper monitors pass out the work sheets.

3. Explain the directions: "To get the answers to these questions, you must walk around the room and talk to every classmate. Being accurate is better than being quick. You'll have about 20 minutes." (The amount of time is up to you. Younger students may need more time or fewer questions.)

4. Give the signal to begin. Circulate around the room, helping, encouraging, keeping students on task, praising work completed, or doing a work sheet yourself.

5. Use your zero-noise signal to indicate when time is up. Have everyone return to his or her seat.

6. Go over each question on the work sheet, asking for a show of hands. For example, "Raise your hand if you have more than 2 pets." "Raise your hand if you have more than 4 pets." Keep asking questions until you find the student with the most pets, and then ask what types of pets he or she has. The objective of this activity is to help students to get to know their classmates and learn about the differences and similarities among them.

Closure: Ask, "Did anyone learn something about a classmate they didn't know before? What?" Be ready to volunteer what you learned about someone or point out a similarity you learned through this activity.

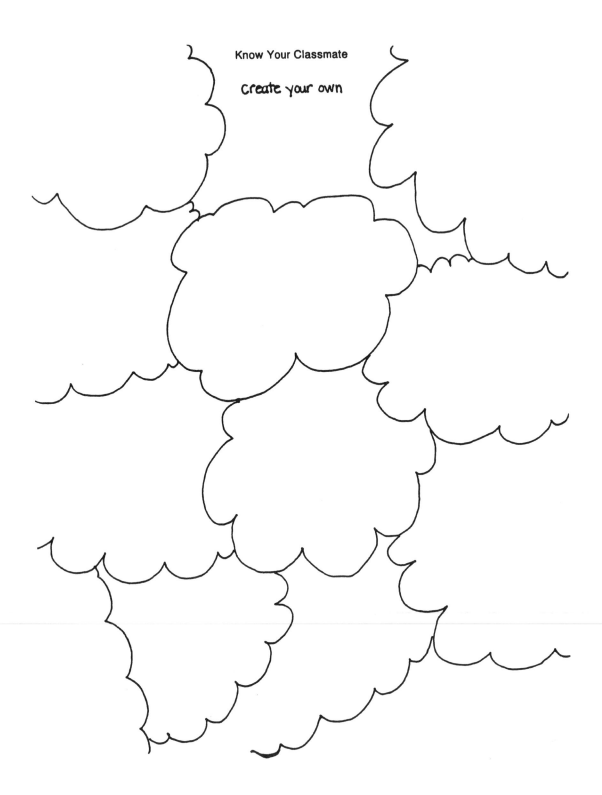

Know Your Classmate

Create your own

Names Games

Action Names

Grouping: whole class

Approximate Time: 45 minutes

Directions:

1. Have students sit in a circle on the floor.

2. Going around the circle, each person gives his or her name with an action for each syllable. For example, Josefina would need 4 syllables. She would say, "Josefina," and then say it again slowly: "Jo"—hits right knee with right hand; "se"—hits left knee with left hand; "fi"—claps hands; "na"—slaps knees with both hands.

3. Have the whole group repeat the motions, saying the name 2 times.

4. Then move on to the next person.

Initial Adjectives

Grouping: cooperative groups

Approximate Time: 30 minutes

Directions:

1. In cooperative groups, come up with an adjective to describe each person that starts with that person's initial; for example, Active Abdul or Jumping Jabar.

2. Have the entire group then create a chant with rhythm motions (clapping, snapping fingers) that includes the names and adjectives of everyone on the team.

3. Have groups simultaneously share their chants.

Name Song

Grouping: whole class

Approximate Time: Variable

Directions: Use the basic name song that follows, and create a song with the names of the students in your class.

Shirley Shirley Bo Birley,

Banana Fana Fo Firley

Fe Fi Mo Mirley, Shirley

Name Scramble

Materials: enough teacher-made work sheets for all students, pencils

Grouping: whole class at desks

Approximate Time: 20 minutes

Directions:

1. Make a work sheet that shows the first names of all students in uppercase letters, with each name scrambled (e.g., Mary might be YARM). Vary the difficulty by

(a) writing the first letter in uppercase and the rest of the name in lowercase, (b) underlining the first letter, and (c) posting a class list for the students to refer to.

2. Explain the directions and behavioral expectations for this activity. Students are to unscramble classmates' names.

3. Pass out the work sheets.

4. While the students work on unscrambling the names, move around the class offering help, listening to conversations, encouraging interactions, and keeping students on task.

5. After 15 minutes, give your zero-noise signal and have students stop working.

6. Go around the room to "correct" the work sheets. Have one person read the first unscrambled name, then another read the second, and so on. Or do simultaneous sharing, with students calling out their responses. You may have each person whose name has been unscrambled stand up, so students can associate name and face.

Closure: Ask, "Which name was the most difficult to unscramble for you and why?" Also ask, "Why would I want you to do an activity like this?" Last, ask, "Who can go around the room and name each person?"

Name Scramble 2

Materials: pencils, scratch paper, teacher-made name strips printed on 8½" × 2" tagboard, with the letters cut apart

Grouping: whole class at desks, then pairs of students

Approximate Time: 45-60 minutes

Directions:

1. Put the cut-up letter pieces for each name in an envelope—one for each name. (To vary the difficulty of this activity, make the pieces larger by cutting between every other letter; make the cuts distinctive, giving visual clues; or place dots on the backs of pieces for last names.)

2. Explain the directions to the class, including behavioral expectations. Students are to reassemble their classmates' names.

3. Randomly distribute the envelopes, making sure that no one receives his or her own name.

4. At your signal, have each student empty his or her envelope and begin to unscramble the mystery name.

5. Once a student completes the unscrambling task, he or she should find the person whose name is on the strip and "interview" him or her.

6. Using their own interview questions (see the following pages for a sample list in English and Spanish), interviewers must learn 5 interesting facts that they will use to introduce the person to the class.

7. Wander around the room to keep everyone on task and to listen to conversations.

8. As the students finish, have them check with you to be sure they have completed all parts of the activity. If they have, tell them to write the unscrambled names of the persons they interviewed on the chalkboard. Use this list for the order of introductions. These 8 steps should take approximately 20 minutes.

9. Have the students sit at their desks or in a class meeting circle for the introductions.

10. As the students introduce each other, listen for and note particularly good questions.

Closure:

1. Discuss the questions and the type of information you would want to know about someone (for instance, "What was one question you thought was particularly good? Why did you like that one? What type of questions help us know more about the person? If you could pick only 5 questions, which ones would you pick?").

2. Record the best questions, to use as a guide for later in the year to get to know new students.

3. You might want to videotape or tape-record the introductions to play back at the end of the school year.

Introducing . . .

_____
(your partner's name)

Ask your partner each question and record his or her comment.

☑ Who are the members in your family? _____

_____

☑ What does your family like to do together? _____

_____

☑ What is something you like to do? _____

_____

☑ Where is your favorite place? Why is it so special? _____

_____

☑ What was the best thing about the summer? _____

_____

☑ I know it's going to be a great school year because _____

_____

☑ One thing I hope we learn about this year is_____

_____

Introduciendo . . .

_____

(nombre de tu pareja)

Hazle estas preguntas a tu pareja y apunta sus respuestas.

_____

☑ ¿Quiénes son los miembros de tu familia? _____

_____

☑ ¿Qué le gusta hacer a tu familia todos juntos? _____

_____

☑ ¿Qué es algo que te gusta hacer? _____

_____

☑ ¿Dónde esta tu lugar favorito? ¿Por qué es tan especial? _____

_____

☑ ¿Qué fue la mejor cosa de tu verano?_____

_____

☑ Yo se que va ser un gran año escolar porque _____

_____

☑ Una cosa que espero que aprendamos este año es _____

_____

Paired Interviews

Materials: paper, pencils
Grouping: partners
Approximate Time: 90 minutes
Directions:

1. Decide as a class on some questions that you would like to ask other people in your class.

2. Pair up and have partners interview each other and write some notes about their partners.

3. Have partners introduce each other in cooperative groups.

4. Have the groups decide on one fact to remember about each person.

5. Have one person in the group summarize the group introduction by telling the class all the group members' names and the one fact about each person.

Closure: Tell the class how impressed you are with such an interesting group of students. Have them take 3 minutes to write down as many interesting facts as they can remember about their classmates.

Significant Object

Materials: paper, pencils, objects brought from home by students
Grouping: partners
Approximate Time: 90 minutes
Directions:

1. Have each student bring something from home that is very important to him or her, some significant object.

2. Follow the procedures for paired interviews, having students interview each other to learn about their significant objects.

Partner Introductions

Materials: index cards
Grouping: partners
Approximate Time: 60 minutes
Directions:

1. Tell the students that to get acquainted with other students in the class, they'll be doing partner introductions. After answering some questions about themselves, students will pair up and introduce each other to the rest of the class.

2. Have paper monitors pass out index cards (one per person). In the middle of these cards, have students write their "special interest nicknames," for example, Adventurous Andrew or Swimming Sandy.

3. In the upper right-hand corner of the card, have each student write the name of his or her favorite place in the world.

4. In the bottom left-hand corner of the card, have each student write down something that is important to him or her.

5. In the top left-hand corner of the card, have each student write something he or she wants to do this year.

6. In the bottom right-hand corner of the card, have each student write something he or she is good at doing.

7. Next, have students pair up and share the information about themselves that they have written. Allow approximately 10-15 minutes for this.

8. Ask for partner volunteers to introduce each other. Encourage students to tell the audience about their partners without reading their cards. This could take from 30 to 45 minutes.

Closure: Ask students, "What was important about this activity? What did you find interesting?"

Please/Please Don't

Materials: two pieces of chart paper, markers
Grouping: whole class
Directions:

1. At the first class meeting, talk with students about the need to come to consensus (agreement) on "how we want to be treated in this classroom."

2. Discuss the process of brainstorming; emphasize the importance of accepting all ideas, with no put-downs or judgments.

3. Question students about why it is important not to judge or put down others' ideas.

4. Set up 2 charts, one labeled "Please . . ." and the other "Please Don't . . ."

5. Ask students to generate endings to these 2 requests (think about whether you want them to yell out or raise their hands beforehand, and explain your chosen procedure before beginning).

6. Discuss the students' comments, as appropriate.

7. Reread the charts at the end of the activity.

Closure: Ask, "Why was it important to talk about this together? What can you do to help your classmates feel safe and comfortable here?"

Day 2: Please/Please Don't
Directions:

1. From looking at the lists made the first day, come up with 4 to 6 rules that would incorporate all of the students' concerns. These rules should be (a) stated in positive terms, (b) broad enough to cover all general behaviors, and (c) stated simply.

2. Transfer the lists that were generated the day before to the board. Explain to the class that you looked at their lists and could see some rules that seemed to cover all of their requests.

3. Write the rules on the board with a lot of space between them. Tell the students that you want to be sure all of their concerns are covered, so you are going to go through their lists together and decide which rule each item would go under.

4. Read the requests on the lists one by one and have the students tell you which rule to put each under. Allow discussion and negotiation. Keep going until all the requests have been covered.

5. Discuss what to do when someone does something on the "Please Don't" list. Have students brainstorm a list of consequences and grade them from mild to severe. Use these rules as guidelines for the class.

Brainstorming: Cheerios

Materials: one box of Cheerios, felt pens, crayons, one piece of butcher paper per group (20" × 30")
Grouping: cooperative groups of 4
Approximate Time: 90 minutes
Directions:

1. Tell the class that this is an activity that will exercise their creative thinking.

2. Divide the class into groups of 4, and then have each group number off, 1 through 4. Assign each number a job: recorder, reporter, timekeeper, and gopher. (Write these on the board for reference.)

3. Talk about what brainstorming is—accepting all ideas, no judgments. Then, tell students they will be working on a creative art activity with Cheerios. First they will brainstorm uses for Cheerios, and then they will do an art project substituting Cheerios for objects in the picture.

4. Have the student groups brainstorm lists of possible uses for Cheerios in a picture (rings, necklaces, wheels for cars, and so on). The group gophers get paper, and the recorders write their groups' ideas. The timekeepers allow 5 minutes for the task.

5. Have the reporters come up front to share 5 of their groups' ideas. Record these ideas on the board for later use in the art project.

6. Now, have the groups work on an art project cooperatively. They will need to decide on a scene and what each person will be responsible for drawing. You may give each one a different color pen to be sure they all contribute. Each group will draw a scene, using Cheerios in place of drawn items as much as possible. For example, a car might have Cheerios as tires. Give approximately 45 minutes for the art project. Gophers distribute Cheerios and butcher paper.

7. Have the groups share and talk about their projects with the class.

Closure: Ask the groups how they decided on their scenes. Ask each group what made its project successful. Ask students within the groups to compliment each other for some specific contributions they made to the project.

Extension: Have the student groups brainstorm analogies (write the words and definitions on the board): "A Cheerio is like a ____ because ____." Talk about the attributes of a Cheerio (shape, size, color, other qualities), and then brainstorm a few analogies as a class. Example: "A Cheerio is like a tire because it's round and has a hole in the middle." Have the recorders report their groups' analogies. Record these on the board.

"Me" Pictures

Materials: tagboard, construction paper, fabric scraps, yarn
Grouping: whole class, individuals
Approximate Time: two 60-minute periods
Directions:

1. Have students create pictures of themselves cut out of construction paper or tagboard, clothing themselves with fabric glued onto backing. When they draw their pictures, tell them to have their heads touch the top of the tagboard and their feet touch the bottom, so that the final pictures don't end up too small. (You should prepare a sample picture of yourself to show to students as an example.) Also, give them the tip that if the arms are too skinny, they'll look funny when they are cut out.

2. Have students add cartoon bubbles to their pictures, showing them saying things they want to tell about themselves.

Closure: Have each student share something he or she likes about his or her neighbor's picture.

Extension: Have students create poems by writing adjectives that begin with each of the letters of their names to put up near their "me" pictures.

Partner Drawings

Materials: colored construction paper, various colors of pastel chalks (2 per student)
Grouping: whole class
Approximate Time: 30-45 minutes
Directions:

1. Have music on quietly in the background.

2. Have students work in partner teams. Make sure each partner has 2 pieces of chalk and that each partnership has one piece of paper. Tell students they may not talk during the art session.

3. One partner starts by drawing any continuous line and stops. The next partner puts his or her chalk on the paper where the last line ended and draws any continuous line and stops. The work goes back and forth until, through nonverbal communication, the partners decide they are finished.

Closure: Ask students, "What did you enjoy about the process? How did you and your partner decide when you were finished? How did you feel about your drawings?"

Variation: Both partners hold one piece of chalk together and create together, still with no talking. For closure on this activity, ask students, "Who was the leader? Did the leadership change? How did you feel?"

Shields

Materials: a shield for each student (make copies of the black-line master on the next page and copy onto 8½ × 11 tagboard or construction paper for final copy), felt pens, crayons

Grouping: individuals

Approximate Time: 45-60 minutes

Directions:

1. Find some pictures of coats of arms or family shields in an encyclopedia. Show these to your students, and tell them that the pictures or emblems in the sections of these shields represent things about that family.

2. Tell students that today they will be making their own shields. They will be getting a shield outline and will need to draw a picture and write a caption in each section. Today, they will be making a practice copy, and tomorrow they will make the final one.

3. Draw a shield on the board and write a label in each section (see the sample on the next page). Students will fill in the shields with pictures or statements (or pictures with captions for each label).

4. Check for understanding, and then have paper monitors pass out the shield blanks. Circulate as the students begin, to be sure they understand what they should be doing.

Closure: Tell the students you will look over their shields that night, help with editing, and return them tomorrow so they can make their final copies. Ask, "Why are family shields important? Did you realize something special about your family as you did this?"

Shields: Day 2

Directions: Return the practice shields and allow time for students to make their final shields on tagboard or white construction paper.

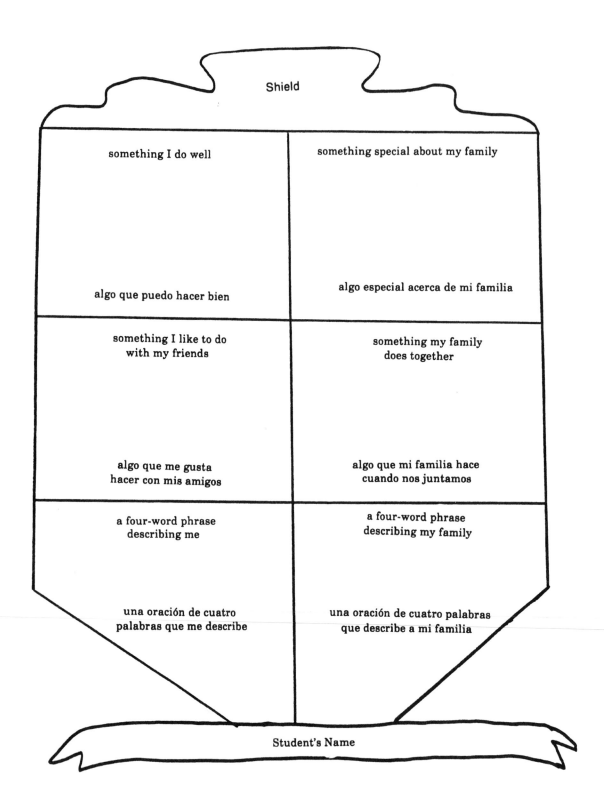

Shield

something I do well	something special about my family
algo que puedo hacer bien	algo especial acerca de mi familia
something I like to do with my friends	something my family does together
algo que me gusta hacer con mis amigos	algo que mi familia hace cuando nos juntamos
a four-word phrase describing me	a four-word phrase describing my family
una oración de cuatro palabras que me describe	una oración de cuatro palabras que describe a mi familia

Student's Name

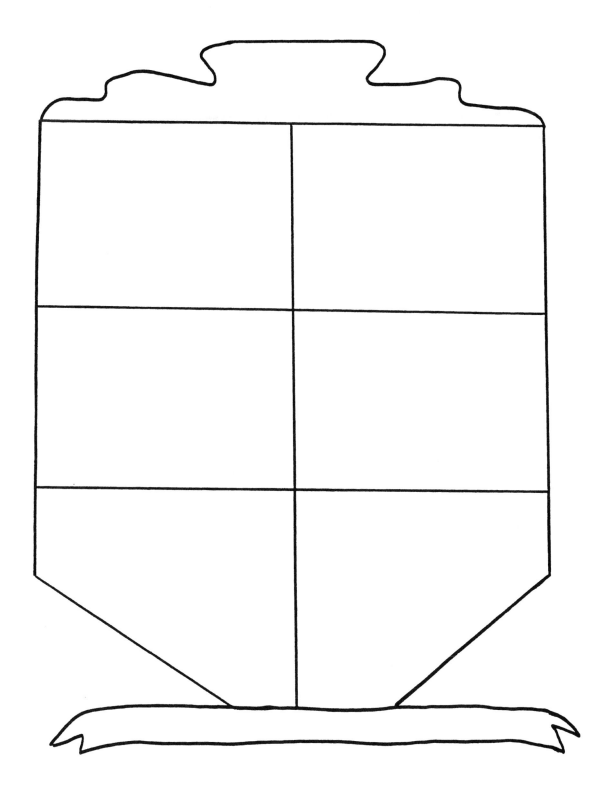

Silhouette Murals

Materials: large white butcher paper sheets covering wall space from floor to ceiling, pencils, projector, chalk, fixative spray, paper towels

Grouping: partners or small groups; rest of class independent (could be practicing individual work with pastel chalks)

Approximate Time: done over a period of a week; best started while the rest of the class works on individual art projects and as a finish-up time project

Directions:

1. Use one or more projectors to project silhouettes of students in various positions on the wall. Draw their outlines in pencil. (Be sure students stand sideways and that their eyelashes show up in their profiles, so they will know where the eyes are.)

2. Start at the top of the paper, with students standing on desks or chairs, and work down the paper to having students kneel or sit. The silhouettes should overlap one another.

3. Help students to draw in hairlines, neck lines, and cheek lines, and then have students color in their own figures with pastel chalks.

4. You can teach the outlining technique to a small team who can help the rest of the students, or an adult can have the responsibility of helping each pair find its spot and get set up to draw. The coloring-in should be a sponge activity for students to work on when they finish other work.

Tips:

1. Have students practice using pastels by coloring in silhouettes on paper at their desks. Demonstrate how they can shade and mix colors with finger-rubbing motions.

2. Have students use paper towels to keep their nondrawing hands from smudging the mural.

3. Have students at the top of the mural color their faces first.

4. Color in all faces before working on hair and clothes, so that no faces get covered.

5. Spray a pastel fixative over the entire mural (do this after school, with all the windows open).

Find Someone Who . . .

Materials: enough work sheets for all students, pencils
Grouping: independent, whole class
Approximate Time: 40 minutes
Directions:

1. Have students put their names on the tops of their work sheets, and then go over the "Someone Who" statements orally so everyone can read them.

2. Have students get as many people as possible to sign their names by the statements that apply to them. Students must ask, "Do you . . .?" or "Have you ever . . .?" before someone can sign their papers. (This is an activity to build language skills as well as get to know one another.)

3. Tell students, "You may sign someone else's paper only once, and others can sign your paper only once each." Review the signal to stop.

4. Call time when a few students are close to finishing their pages.

Closure: Discuss who signed for each of the statements. You might want to graph the results. Ask students what they learned about their classmates.

Name _____

Find someone who . . .

Has 3 brothers _____

Likes tortillas _____

Plays baseball _____

Likes to dance _____

Was born in another country _____

Likes rock music _____

Has read *Ramona the Pest* _____

Eats cereal for breakfast _____

Walks to school _____

Can speak a language other than English _____

Has a cat for a pet _____

Has ridden a horse _____

Has a truck in the family _____

Has a baby in the family _____

Has long hair _____

Has a fireplace in his or her house _____

Nombre _____

Encuentra a una persona que . . .

Tiene tres hermanos _____

Le gustan las tortillas _____

Juega baseball _____

Le gusta bailar _____

Nació en otro país _____

Le gusta la música rock _____

Ha leído *Ramona la Chinche* _____

Come cereal en el desayuno _____

Camina a la escuela _____

Puede hablar otro idioma además de Inglés _____

Tiene un gato mascota _____

Ha montado un caballo _____

Tiene un camión en su familia _____

Tiene un bebé en su familia _____

Tiene el cabello largo _____

Tiene una chiminea en su casa _____

Graffiti Boards

Materials: butcher paper cut into 15" × 36" pieces, glue, staplers, felt pens
Grouping: individual
Approximate Time: 45 minutes
Directions:

1. As homework the night before, ask students to bring in "3 things from home that represent you and are important to you" to hang on a chart. Give examples: pictures, special clothing, awards, book jackets, and so on.

2. Pass out the pieces of butcher paper and have the students write their names in large letters across the top, and then glue or staple their items onto the paper. Explain what graffiti boards are and that graffiti can be an art form, but if written on buildings, it can be a form of vandalism. Have a discussion about this.

3. Display the graffiti boards on the bulletin board. Encourage students to write specific positive comments (model these, as well as nonspecific or inappropriate comments) on each others' graffiti boards during free time or independent work time.

4. Discuss how someone might feel if his or her board had no comments. Ask the group to come up with a system to ensure that this does not happen.

Closure: Ask, "How did this activity make you feel? How might it be useful to our class as a whole? To individuals?"

Letters

Materials: writing paper, pencils, enough teacher-written letters for all students, an envelope for each letter

Grouping: whole class, individual

Approximate Time: 20-30 minutes

Directions:

1. Before this class session, write a letter, leaving the name of the addressee blank. Make it friendly and chatty. In the letter, tell about yourself, what you like, your hobbies, and so on. You could include major units you have planned and ask for students' thoughts about school. At the end of the letter, ask them to write back to you, telling about themselves. Make enough copies for all your students. Before delivering the letters, address them individually with the students' names and put them in envelopes, also addressed individually.

2. Pass out the letters. Generally, students' curiosity is piqued by this, and they begin without a lot of direction. If they don't begin working silently after 2-3 minutes, remind them of the procedures for independent work. Tell them they will have about 20 minutes to write their letters (this will vary with the grade level of the class). Tell them what they may do if they finish early (read a book, do a special work sheet you have ready, or whatever). Circulate to keep students on task and to encourage those who have a hard time starting.

3. When you see that everyone has finished, collect the letters and express your interest in reading them. (Save the letters to use in your student assessments; see Chapter 6.)

Quote Discussion

Materials: a meaningful quote, paper, pencils
Grouping: variable (groups of 4, individual, or whole class)
Directions:

1. Write a meaningful quote on the board.

2. Ask students to discuss what the quote means in cooperative groups.

3. Ask individuals to write down the quote, tell what it means, and give personal examples of how the quote applies to their own lives.

4. Form a large circle and discuss what the quote means (no judgments) to different people.

Closure: Ask the class, "What did you learn from this discussion?"

Extensions: This can be used as a homework assignment. Ask students to discuss the quote at home, at the dinner table, and report back.

Famous Quotations
"Whether you think you can or think you can't—you are right."
Henry Ford

"If it is to be . . . It is up to me."
William Johnson

"Everyone has a fair turn to be as great as he pleases."
Jeremy Collier

"No one can make you feel inferior without your permission."
Eleanor Roosevelt

"It's not so much what you do that makes you special . . . It's who you are."
Anonymous

"Every job is a self-portrait of the person who did it. Autograph your work with excellence."
Anonymous

"The secret to success in any human endeavor is concentration."
Kurt Vonnegut

"Nothing great was ever achieved without enthusiasm."
Ralph Waldo Emerson

"If you're not part of the solution, you're part of the problem."
M. Scott Peck

Dichos Famosos

"Si crees que puedes o si crees que no puedes—tienes razón."
Henry Ford

"Si algo ha de ser . . . ha de ser de mi voluntad."
William Johnson

"No es tanto lo que haces que te valora, si no quien eres."
AnÓnimo

"El secreto del éxito en cualquier empeño humano es la concentración."
Kurt Vonnegut

"Sin entusiasmo, ninguno de los grandes hechos se hubieran llevado a cabo."
Ralph Waldo Emerson

"Si tu no eres parte de la solución, eres parte del problema."
M. Scott Peck

"El respeto al derecho ajeno, es la paz."
Benito Juarez

Wiggly Line Drawing

Materials: enough work sheets for all students, pencils or crayons
Grouping: independent
Approximate Time: 45 minutes
Directions:

1. Place Wiggly Line work sheets and pencils or crayons on desks so that when students come in, they can do this as a transition activity.

2. Tell students to look at the work sheet and follow the instructions. As they are working, roam around the class to answer any questions and provide encouragement. Note anyone having trouble reading the directions or getting started writing.

3. As students finish their work, be ready to put all of the work sheets directly up on the wall as a display of their drawing and writing.

4. Look at the writing samples to note where each student is developmentally in his or her writing skills. Save these samples to use in one of your initial assessments.

Closure: Read a few of the Wiggly Line stories to the class each day until they have all been shared. Ask the class to share some things they liked.

*White out several of the writing lines for second and third graders. This will give the students more space for their drawings.

Name _____/ Date_____

Wiggly Line/Línea Ondulada
Use this line to begin a picture. Then write a story about your picture.
Usa esta línea para comenzar un dibujo. Escribe un cuento sobre su dibujo.

Math Challenges

Materials: math journals, pencils
Grouping: individual
Approximate Time: 15-20 minutes
Directions:

1. Begin the math period with a brief challenge activity. Have a place on the board where the math challenge is written each day, so students can get started when they come in. The challenge might be from any of the math strands, or it might focus on the computational process you are currently teaching. You might want to make up math problems using information that is relevant to your class or that fits in with what you are studying in other content areas (e.g., if you're studying marine life, your problems could be about otters, fish, and so on).

2. Have students work the math challenge problem in their math journals (see Math Journal activity, described later).

3. When the time is up, discuss the various strategies students used to solve the problem. Have several students come to the board to share their diagrams and equations and tell about the various strategies they used to solve the problem. Encourage the students to draw pictures to show their solutions and have them write equations to explain their computations.

Examples of Challenges

1. How much will a dozen 6-cent stamps cost? ($12 \times \$.06 = \$.72$)

2. There are 11 clothespins strung on a line. Each clothespin is 6 centimeters from the previous clothespin. How many centimeters is it from the first clothespin to the last clothespin? ($6 \times 10 = 60$ cm.)

3. If eggs cost 96 cents a dozen, how many eggs can you by for 3 quarters, 2 dimes, and 1 penny? ($\$.75 + \$.20 + \$.01 = \$.96$; 1 dozen)

4. One place charges $39.00 a day to rent a car. Another place charges $58.00 a day. How much can you save by renting the car from the first place rather than the second? ($\$58.00 - \$39.00 = \$19.00$)

5. Mom has 4 pies. She wants to cut them so each of 8 people has the same size piece. What is the size of each piece? ($4 \div 8 = \frac{1}{2}$ pie for each piece)

6. Rosa had ____ rose bushes. She went to the garden shop and bought 9 more. How many plants did she buy if she has 21 in all? ($21 - 9 = 12$)

7. Estimate how many shoelace holes are in our class today.

8. Apples cost 43 cents a pound. How many pounds of apples did I buy if I spent $2.15? ($\$2.15 \div 43 = 5$ lbs.)

En Español

1. ¿Cuánto cuesta una docena de timbres de seis centavos? (12 × $.06 = $.72)

2. Once ganchos están en la linea. Cada gancho está a seis centimetros de cada uno. ¿Cuántos cent¡metros hay del primer gancho al último? (6 × 10 = 60 cm)

3. ¿Si una docena de blanquillos cuesta 96 centavos, cuántos blanquillos puedes comprar con 3 "quarters," 2 "dimes," y 1 centavo? ($.75 + $.20 + $.01 = $.96; 1 docena)

4. En un lugar cobran $39.00 al día por rentar un carro. Otro lugar cobra $58.00 al día. ¿Cuánto puedes ahorrar si rentas el carro en el primer lugar en lugar del segundo lugar? ($58.00 – $39.00 = $19.00)

5. Una madre tiene 4 pasteles. Ella quiere cortar 8 pedazos para que cada persona ténga pedazos del mismo tamaño. ¿Cuál es el tamaño de cada pedazo? (½ pastel para cada uno)

6. Rosa tenía _____ rosales. Ella fuî a la jardiner¡a y compró 9 más. ¿Cuántos rosales compró si tenía 21 en total? (21 – 9 = 12 rosales)

7. ¿Asproximadamente, cuántos hojillos hay en todos los zapatos en la clase?

8. Las manzanas cuestan 43 centavos la libra. ¿Cuántas libras de manzanas compr, hoy si gasté $2.15? ($2.15 + 43 = 5 lbs.)

The Class Age

Materials: calculators (if possible, 1 for every 2 students)
Grouping: partners
Approximate Time: 30-40 minutes
Directions:

1. Have each student guess what the sum of everyone's age will be. Record the estimates on the board.

2. Give each set of partners a calculator. If this is their first time with calculators, give students some time to play around with them; let them know what is acceptable and what is not. Go over the functions of the keys and do a couple of practice problems. Also go over the care and handling of a calculator.

3. Review teacher-led lesson procedures.

4. Go around the class, asking each student how old he or she is. Have the partners enter each age in their calculators and then push the plus key. Ask for a subtotal after each entry. If any pair has made an error, they can clear the calculator and start again with the correct subtotal.

5. Compare the results with the estimates.

Extensions:

1. Graph this activity.

2. Do this activity with other attributes, such as the combined heights of class members. Or how long a line would the class make if all the students lay down head to toe? Older students could also find the average, range, and median age, height, or whatever.

Cooperative Triangles

Materials: enough copies of the cooperative triangle (see next page) for all students, crayons, pencils, felt pens

Grouping: cooperative groups of 3

Approximate Time: 30 minutes

Directions:

1. Have students work in groups of 3 to count all the triangles in the figure. Assign group jobs: recorder, reporter, and facilitator (checks for agreement, keeps discussion going, makes sure everyone participates).

2. Each group must come up with a strategy for keeping track of the triangles counted.

3. Give approximately 5 minutes for the task.

4. Have the reporters share their groups' findings. Have facilitators tell about the strategies their groups used in keeping track of the triangles.

Closure: Come to consensus, if possible. There is no need to tell the answer; some students will pursue the problem.

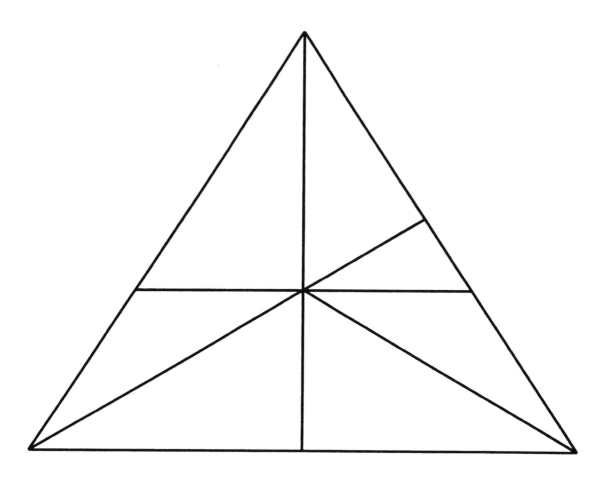

Problem-Solving Strategies: Estimating Raisins

Materials: construction paper, scrap paper, crayons, felt pens, 1 half-ounce box of raisins for each cooperative group

Grouping: cooperative groups of 4

Approximate Time: 30 minutes

Directions:

1. Write the following directions on the board:
   - (a) As a group, estimate how many raisins are in a half-ounce box.
   - (b) Write the estimate and tell how you came up with it. Recorder writes group's ideas.
   - (c) Open the box and count how many raisins are in it. Determine a strategy for counting them quickly.
   - (d) Write the number of actual raisins in your box, and tell the difference between the estimated and actual number of raisins.
   - (e) Divide the raisins equally among the members of your group.
   - (f) Draw a picture of each member's share of raisins.
   - (g) Write an equation or number sentence for dividing the raisins.

2. Explain to the students that they will be working in cooperative groups. Each person will have a role: The gopher will distribute and collect the materials; the recorder will write down what group members say; the leader will make sure everyone participates equally, using positive praise; and the timekeeper will keep the group on task and on time. Assign roles to students by having them number off and making all Number 1s gophers and so on.

3. Read over the directions written on the board, modeling an example of how the task might be done and reviewing what each of the roles might look like during the process. Review cooperative group procedures with the class.

4. Explain that when the groups finish, they will all have group sheets that explain the process of how they solved the problem. These group sheets will all be put into a class book.

Closure: When their group sheet has been turned in, have each group discuss and write how they divided up the task and what made the group work well.

Evaluation: Gather on the rug and discuss what criteria should be evaluated: neatness-organization, content, correctness, enhancements. Go through all of the group sheets and evaluate them together against the chosen criteria (you might assign 10 points to each area). In this way, you will model evaluation for the class for future journal entries. You may graph your results.

Math Journal

Materials: folders for all students with graph or grid paper stapled inside, pencils
Grouping: whole class, individual
Approximate Time: variable
Directions:

1. Explain to your students that math journals are places where they write about how to solve math problems. They provide students with an opportunity to think through their strategies for solving problems so that they may apply those strategies in other situations. (These journals also provide you with valuable information on students' problem-solving skills. They are also a great way to integrate math and writing skills and to develop expository writing skills.)

2. Use the raisin estimation activity to have students begin the process of math journals in a cooperative setting. After the activity, explain that the students' journals will be evaluated in the same way the class book was.

3. Give each student a folder with graph or grid paper stapled inside to use as a math journal. Have the students begin their journals by reflecting on the process of doing math cooperatively in the raisin estimation activity. Ask, "What do you like about doing math cooperatively, compared with doing it alone?" Discuss and share some entries from volunteers.

4. Use journals a few times a month as an in-depth project. Have students explain and illustrate the process of solving a problem.

5. Use journals daily to work on or record math challenge problems.

6. Have students use the journals also to record their feelings about math and to create their own math problem stories. Have students reflect on their experience in math and what they have learned or what they are having difficulty with.

Assessment: Collect 6 to 8 journals each week to assess (everyone is assessed monthly). Skim through and make some notes in your anecdotal record log about students' thinking skills (logical, sequential, organizational strategies). Use the criteria the class decided on for evaluation (neatness, content, correctness, enhancements). You may want to photocopy a page or two of each student's journal to keep in his or her math folder to show thinking skills to parents or to show strengths or weaknesses in strategies.

Graphing

Materials: paper, pencils, pens, graph paper, chart paper
Grouping: partners
Approximate Time: 45 minutes
Directions:

1. Have the students work in pairs. Pair them up ahead of time: have them count off or let them self-select their partners.

2. Discuss the types of questions the class used in Partner Introductions to get to know their classmates. Record the questions on the board.

3. Have each pair of students select a question, or assign a question to each pair.

4. Let the pairs work together to decide the type of graph they want to make and how they should record the information. Review various types of graphs and have samples of each available. For younger students, decide the type of graph they should use and teach them how to collect the data.

5. Give the class 10 minutes to move around the room to get the data for their graphs.

6. Have students return to their seats to begin work on their graphs. Supply pens, graph paper, and chart paper. While the students are working, encourage them to work together and to do their best work on the graphs. Mention some elements of a useful graph: a title, clearly labeled information, legibility, and so on.

7. When the graphs are complete, have each pair write a sentence explaining what their graph says. Display the graphs in the room as a student-made bulletin board.

Extension: Have students create surveys to take home and use to survey 5 people. Have them create graphs using the new information with their partners the next day.

People Measuring

Materials: enough pieces of string for all students to have several (cut each piece longer than the tallest student in the class), masking tape, pencils

Grouping: partners

Approximate Time: 30-40 minutes

Directions:

1. Go over the procedures for a teacher-led lesson with small groups.

2. Have students pair up. You can assign partners ahead of time or have the students number off. The important part is that no one feels left out and that everyone has a partner.

3. Pass out several pieces of string to each student. (Older students could do this activity using meter sticks or tape measures.)

4. First, have the students, in pairs, help each other measure and cut their pieces of string to the exact height of their partners. Then, have them measure each others' arm spans and cut strings to that length. Give the students time to complete the measuring (and recording, for older students) while you circulate. Give them masking tape to label which body part each piece of string represents; have them initial their labels. The students may continue measuring arms, legs, head circumference, and so on in the same way.

5. Have the students graph their findings in one or more of the following ways. Tape all the strings representing height, arm span, and so on along a wall on a piece of masking tape to see all the different lengths, creating a string graph. Have students measure their strings with rulers, convert their measurements from feet and inches to meters and centimeters, and graph the class.

6. Have students look at relationships between height and arm span or height and head circumference, and so on, making predictions and testing them out. Record the results and compare what they find. Have them tell how their measurements compare; for example, "My height is 3 times the circumference of my head."

Homework Ideas

Whenever possible, homework should reinforce in-class work or prepare students for a coming lesson. Part of the purpose of homework is to teach study habits at home. It is important to discuss with students how they might set up a routine to get homework done and put in a special place so they will remember to bring it back. There should be a basket near the classroom door for turning in homework. It can be checked in quickly by an instructional aide or a student. Assigning numbers to be placed in the upper left-hand corners of papers, which correspond to a class record list, will facilitate putting papers in order to check off. Send a letter home to parents to inform them of the homework schedule. (See Chapter 7 for a sample.)

Ideas for Homework Assignments

- ☑ Read silently or to a brother, sister, or parent for 30 minutes (this can be signed off in a notebook by a parent).
- ☑ Write a story based on a story starter, such as "The worst day of my life . . . " or "The best party I can imagine . . . "
- ☑ Study math facts related to current in-class math work.
- ☑ Walk through your house or neighborhood looking for all the things whose names start with a certain letter, particular sounds, particular smells, things using electricity, things that are living, things that come from different countries, and so on.
- ☑ Interview family members on different issues.
- ☑ Look for all the pictures, television shows, foods, fabrics, colors, and so on that relate to a particular thematic unit coming up in class.
- ☑ Survey neighbors, friends, and family to graph the next day.
- ☑ Write about or draw who lives in your house, including at least 2 adjectives about each person.
- ☑ Draw the name of a classmate from a hat in class, and write a description of that person to use in a "guess who" game.
- ☑ Write a letter to a relative, a political leader, or a company to bring in for editing and revision.

Sponge Activities

Sponge activities are so named because they soak up time. They should be fun activities that can be done spontaneously, enhancing learning in subtle ways. Ask your class to brainstorm their favorite games from previous years and keep a list. Have students model the games for the rest of the class when you are ready to play. Some ideas they will probably come up with are Around the World, Multiplication Baseball, and Heads-Up 7-Up.

Reliable Sponge Activities

People Sorting: Think of a rule in your mind, such as students with short sleeves. Call students to come and stand next to you in front of the class. Those that follow the rule (who are wearing short sleeves) stand on your right; others stand on your left. Ask the class if they can guess your rule. Any students who think they know the rule must tell you which side they should stand on. Keep sorting students until you think many people know the rule, then ask them to say what they think your rule is. This is very good for vocabulary development (for learning such words as denim, velcro, collars, pullovers, jewelry, beige).

Lineups: Have the whole class line up around the room in some of the following ways: in order of birth dates, alphabetical order by first or last name, distance they live from the school, farthest point they've ever traveled to, shortest to tallest. Variation: Pass out pictures to use for fastest to slowest transportation, biggest to smallest animal, and so on. Ask students to share what they learned during this activity. Ask what other ways they might line up.

Mastermind: Students try to guess a word you're thinking of by guessing letters. They get an X for each right letter in the right place. They get an O for a right letter but in the wrong place, and they get a dash for a wrong letter. They try to use the fewest guesses possible.

20 Questions: Have the students try to guess something you are thinking of by asking only yes-or-no questions. They have 20 questions. Teach the students some questioning strategies that start out in broad categories and narrow down, such as "Is it animal, vegetable, or mineral?" (This is a "free" question, and the only non-yes-no question allowed.) If animal, "Is it a reptile?" If no, "Is it a mammal?" If yes, "Does it live on land?" If no, "Does it live in water?" And so on. One variation on this game is to have students guess a number rather than an object. Encourage them to use terms such as *greater than, less than, odd, even, a multiple of, in the 60s.* Another variation uses careers (What's My Line?). Instead of just yes-or-no questions, students can ask, "Would you . . . " questions, with possible answers being "every day," "sometimes," "hardly ever," and "never."

Wonderball: While passing a ball around a circle, the class chants,
"The wonderball goes round and round, / to pass it quickly you are bound. / If you're the one to hold it last, / then for you, the game has passed." The one holding the ball when the chant ends is out. Keep rounds short, so students can get back into the game.

Switch: Two students go out of the room while everyone else changes seats. When the 2 come back in, they must return misplaced students to their correct desks within 3 minutes. (Remove student name cards from desks.)

Clap Action: One student goes out of the room, and the rest of the class decides on an action, such as washing hands or touching the chalkboard. The student returns and tries to guess the action by moving to different areas of the room and trying out different movements. The class guides him or her by clapping louder and louder as the student gets closer to the correct task. A variation on this game, *You're Hot,* has students call out "You're getting warmer" (moving toward it) or "You're getting colder" (moving away from it) as a student tries to find a hidden object.

Categories: Sitting with the class in a circle, start a rhythm of clapping and hitting knees. Choose a category (for instance, presidents) and say, "Categories, presidents." Then, each person in turn around the circle has to name a president before 2 rhythm claps have gone by, or they are out. There are many other categories you can use, such as fruits, domestic animals, words beginning with a certain letter, authors, television shows, and adjectives.

Safari: Decide on a category of attributes (in this example, things with 4 legs) that will be the same about all the things you are taking on an imaginary safari; tell students they can come with you if they bring the correct kinds of items. You say, "I'm going on a safari and I'm taking an elephant and a chair." If a student wants to go on safari with you, he or she must say, "I'm going with you, and I'm bringing a table (or a dog, or a something else that has 4 legs)." Students who name the right kinds of items then get up and stand with you in front of the class. If a student wants to bring the wrong kind of item, you say, "Sorry, you can't come." You can vary this game by using other kinds of trips (picnics, vacations) and by using beginning-letter sounds, 2-syllable words, or other attributes of the words rather than the objects.

My Aunt Likes Coffee, But She Doesn't Like Tea: Write a couple of items on the board that follow a pattern. Students have to guess other things that fit into the pattern of something "your aunt" would like. For example, using beginning letter sounds, she might like cookies, cakes, coffee, and camping, but not pies, turnovers, tea, or backpacking. As with Safari, you can vary this game by using different patterns: word-ending sounds, number of syllables, and so on.

Function Machine: Draw a picture of or create a 3-dimensional function machine that you can put numbers into and change them to something else. The functions can get more and more complex as students get better at the game. Example: "I put in 3 and out comes 9, I put in 6 and out comes 12. What is the function?" (Add 6.) "I put in a 3 and out comes 10, I put in a 4 and out comes 13, I put in a 5 and out comes 16. What is the function?" (Multiply by 3 and add 1.)

PE Ideas

Think out your procedures for each game. Explain any new games prior to leaving the classroom, using drawings on the chalkboard if necessary. Explain to the class the proper dress for PE—tennis shoes and shorts or pants. Remind students of the attention signal to be used outside. Allow 2 minutes for students to change and meet the class outside. Set the procedures for choosing teams, if necessary, and remind students about the "no put-down" rule. For team games, either you or team captains should choose equal teams at another time to be ready for PE. Vary the types of activities so that not just the athletically inclined enjoy success at PE time.

Besides the following suggested games, relay races, four square, kickball, softball, soccer, and basketball are old standbys that your students will be wanting to learn.

Steal the Bacon: Create 2 lines and have them both number off so each student has a number; have the lines stand opposite each other, with some space in between. When you call out a number, those students who have that number run out, steal the "bacon" (chalkboard eraser) from the center, and run back over their lines. The one who makes it first gets a point.

Steal the Basket: This is the same as Steal the Bacon, but the students steal a basketball, dribble, and try to make a basket.

Knots: Divide the class into 3 groups. Each group forms a circle, shoulder to shoulder, and then each student grabs hands with anyone who is not standing next to him or her. Each student must hold the hands of 2 different people. When these "knots" are all tied, the groups try to untangle the mess without ever letting go of hands. Students must step over and under, twist and turn, but never drop a hand. If a group comes to a deadlock, the teacher may make 1 break to help them move on. (This and the next game are from *The New Games Book,* by Andrew Fluegelman.)

The Lap Game: Form a circle with everyone facing in one direction. One person lies down, with knees bent and feet flat on the ground. The next person sits down on the first person's knees, forming an easy-chair "lap" for the next person to sit in. This proceeds around the circle until everyone is sitting on each others' laps. The hard part is hoisting up the person who formed the initial lap to sit on the person behind.

T-Ball: This is a noncompetitive form of baseball, good for young beginners to practice their skills. Set 2 teams up just as in baseball, but instead of getting outs, each student gets a turn at bat and then you change sides. There is no pitcher; the ball is placed on a tee for the batter to swing at. Don't keep track of runs—this game is just for fun and practice.

Tag Games

These games are noncompetitive and get the class involved and moving. In such games, the object is to *not* be tagged by the person who is IT. Rather than playing one con-

Moran, C., Stobbe, J., Baron, W., Miller, J., & Moir, E. Keys to the Classroom, Second Edition. Copyright © 2000, Corwin Press, Inc.

tinuous game where only one student is IT, stop play after 7-10 minutes. Choose someone new to be IT; repeat the game.

Octopus Tag

Designate a play area. Class lines up on one side; then, on your signal, runs to the other side. One or more students may be the Octopus who runs around in the middle, trying to tag runners as they run from one side to the other. When a runner is tagged, that person becomes a Tentacle and tries to tag others. Tentacles cannot move from the place where they were tagged—instead, they reach out as the runners run by.

Freeze Tag

Start with the basic set-up as in Octopus Tag. This time, when the person who is IT tags a runner, the runner freezes where he or she was tagged. Other runners help frozen players by crawling through their legs to unfreeze them so they can continue to play.

Blob Tag

Start as with Octopus Tag. The player who is IT tags runners as they run from one side to another of the area. Now, when someone is tagged, he or she holds hands with the person who is IT and together they run to tag other players. As more are tagged and the blob extends, pairs may break off to continue running after others. Game ends when all players have become part of the blob or when too exhausted to proceed.

Color Tag

Start with basic set-up. Whoever is IT stands in the center and calls out a color. All who are wearing that color walk to the other side. Everyone else runs while the player who is IT tries tagging him or her before they reach the other side. If a player is tagged, he or she remains in that spot, trying to tag other runners as they go by, without moving the position of their feet.

Touch Down

Designate a playing area with one team lined up on one side, the opposing team on the other. Choose one team to *huddle*, so the opposition cannot see their hands. Place a piece of chalk in one player's hands. All team members should pretend they have the chalk. The chosen team gets ready and lines up. When teacher blows the whistle, both teams run toward each other. Team holding the chalk tries to cross the opposing team's line, while that team tries to prevent them by tagging their players. When a player is tagged, he or she must stop and show what they are holding. If the player holding the chalk is tagged, the play is over with no point scored. If the player with the chalk makes it over the line, that team scores a point. Alternate teams so each has a chance to carry the chalk. This is a fast-paced game!

6

Fingerplays and Songs for Oral Language in English and Spanish

Fingerplays and songs are excellent for oral language development in primary grades. They are also very effective for second-language learning at any age. The interaction of visual cues, kinesthetic movements, and comprehensible language combined with rhythm makes them easily committed to memory. They can be used to build a base of common vocabulary in your class. They are also wonderful transition activities or sponges to bring students together and get them ready for the next activity.

CHAPTER CONTENTS ◆

ATTENTION-GETTING FINGERPLAYS

These fingerplays are those you should start when you need the group's attention. Learn at least 2 or 3 to use the first week of school, then add one each week. You will find you use them all year.

Good Morning
(sung to the tune of "Are You Sleeping?")

Good morning, good morning.
How are you? How are you?
Very well, thank you.
Very well, thank you.
How are you? How are you?

Buenos Días
Buenos días, buenos días.
¿Cómo está? ¿Cómo está?
Muy bien, gracias.
Muy bien, gracias.
¿Y usted? ¿Y usted?

Open Them, Shut Them
Open them, shut them. [hands]
Open them, shut them.
Give your hands a clap.
Open them, shut them.
Open them, shut them.
Fold them in your lap.

Abranlas, Ciérrenlas (chant)
Abranlas, ciérrenlas.
Abranlas, ciérrenlas.
Pla, pla, pla.
Abranlas, ciérrenlas.
Abranlas, ciérrenlas.
Pónganlas acá.

One Little Eye (chant)
One little eye goes wink, wink, wink.
Two little eyes go blink, blink, blink.
One little hand goes snap, snap, snap.
Two little hands go clap, clap, clap.
Now fold them quietly in your lap.

Head, Shoulders, Knees, and Toes
(This song may be done first in normal rhythm, then slow motion, then fast motion, to get lots of energy out.)

Head and shoulders, knees and
  toes,
Knees and toes.
Head and shoulders, knees and
  toes,
Knees and toes.
Eyes and ears and mouth and nose,
Head and shoulders, knees and
  toes,
Knees and toes.

De Cabeza a los Dedos
Cabeza, hombros, rodillas y dedos,
Rodillas y dedos.
Cabeza, hombros, rodillas y dedos,
Rodillas y dedos.
Ojos, orejas, boca, y nariz,
Cabeza, hombros, rodillas y dedos,
Rodillas y dedos.

Two Little Hands
(sung to the tune of "Ten Little Indians")

Two little hands, ten little fingers.
  (Hold up two fists, then show ten
  fingers.)
Two little hands, ten little fingers.
Two little hands, ten little fingers.
Count them all with me.
One little, two little, three little
  fingers.
Four little, five little, six little
  fingers.
Seven little, eight little, nine little
  fingers.
We all have ten fingers.

Dos Manitas
(sung to the tune of "Ten Little Indians")

Dos manitas, diez deditos,
Dos manitas, diez deditos,
Dos manitas, diez deditos,
Cuéntenlos conmingo,
Uno, dos, tres deditos
Cuatro, cinco, seis deditos
Siete, ocho, nueve deditos
Diez deditos tengo.

In Spanish, the same tune can be sung using colors:
Rojo, verde, amarillo.
Blanco, negro, anaranjado,
Gris, café azul, morado,
¡Diez colores tengo!

How Many Fingers?
Do you know? Do you know?
How many fingers I'm going to show?

(Show a number of fingers. Group counts and responds.)

Retintín
Retintín, retintón
¿Cúantos, cúantos dedos son?

Touch
Touch your shoulders,
Touch your knees,
Raise your arms,
Then drop them please.
Touch your ankles,
Then touch your toes,
Pull your ears,
Then touch your nose.
With your toes go
Tap, tap, tap.
Now your fingers
Snap, snap, snap.
Stretch as high as high can be.
While you're there,
Clap one two, three.

Toca
Mis hombritos, mis rodillas,
Así extiendo mis brazitos,
Mis tobillos, y mis pies,
Mis oidos, enseño diez (dedos).
Con mis pies me paro así,
Y mis dedos trueno así.
Luego yo me estiro pues,
Y aplaudo uno, dos, tres.

Where Is Thumbkin?
Where is Thumbkin?
Where is Thumbkin?
Here I am.
Here I am.
How are you today, sir?
Very well I thank you.
Run away, run away.

Repeat, substituting for the first two lines:

Where is Pointer?
Where is Tall Finger?
Where is Ring Finger?
Where is Little Finger?
Where is everybody?

Mi Cuerpo y Yo
Yo me levanto, estoy de pie.
Cuento los dedos, uno, dos, tres.
Abro la boca, cierro los ojos.
Me toco los labios que son rosas.
Giro a la derecha, estoy contento,
Saco la lengua por un momento.
Abro los ojos, miro al cielo.
Me toco la cabeza, cubierto de pelo,
Doy palmadas, levanto el brazo.
Giro a la izquierda y doy un paso.

INCLUSION SONGS

These songs either use the children's own names or involve the group in making up new verses. In these ways, they help the children feel part of the class.

The More We Get Together
The more we get together, together, together,
The more we get together,
The happier you'll be.
There's [child's name] and [child's name] [continue to name children as they are ready, or you want to excuse them to line, or whatever]
The happier you'll be.

Lo Más Que nos Juntamos
Lo más que nos juntamos, juntamos, juntamos,
Lo más que nos juntamos,
Más contento/a estoy.
Hay [nombre de un niño] y [otro nombre] [diga los nombres de los niños que estan listos, o para dejar a unos irse a la fila, o por cualquier razón]
Más contento/a estoy.

If You're Happy and You Know It
If you're happy and you know it, clap your hands.
If you're happy and you know it, clap your hands.
If you're happy and you know it,
Then your face will surely show it.
If you're happy and you know it, clap your hands.
If you're happy and you know it, tap your foot.
If you're happy and you know it, tap your foot.
If you're happy and you know it,
Then your face will surely show it.
If you're happy and you know it, tap your foot.
    (Ask the children to give other motions. Sing each.)

Cuando Tengas Muchas Ganas
(adaptación en español por Silvia Padilla)

Cuando tengas muchas ganas de aplaudir.
Cuando tengas muchas ganas de aplaudir.
Cuando tengas la ilusión y no hay intervención no te quedes con las ganas de aplaudir.
Cuando tengas muchas ganas de brincar.
Cunado tengas muchas ganas de brincar.
Cuando tengas la ilusión y no hay intervención no te quedes con las ganas de brincar.

(Change the verb for each new verse to do new actions or to practice letter sounds (e.g., cepillar—ch, ch; beber—g, g; comer—m,m)

An adaptation of If You're Happy and You Know It/Cuando Tengas Muchas Ganas follows. Use this to develop phonemic awareness.

If you think you know the word, tell me it. (Clap, clap)
If you think you know the word, tell me it. (Clap, clap)
If you think you know the word, if you think you know the word, if you think you
   know the word, tell me it. (Clap, clap) /d/ /o/ /g/
Si tu sabes la palabra-dímela. (Clap, clap)
Si tu sabes la palabra-dímela. (Clap, clap)
Si tu sabes la palabra, si tu sabes la palabra, si tu sabes la palabra, dímela. (Clap, clap)
   /r/ /a/ /n/ /a/

Cookie Jar

Group: Who stole the cookie from the cookie jar?
[Name of child] stole the cookie from the cookie jar.
Individual: Who me?
Group: Yes, you!
Individual: Couldn't be!
Group: Then who?
Individual: [Name of another child.] (Group begins the chant again with that child's
   name and so on.)

Rhythm Chant

Start a snap, clap, slap knees rhythm. Have the children join with you. Then, on each snap, say a child's name. Go around the group, saying each child's name in turn. For example: clap, slap knees, José (snap while saying José); clap, slap knees, María; clap, slap knees, Wendy; and so on.

Sally Go Round the Sun

As the group sings this song, one child skips around the outside of the circle (substitute that child's name for "Sally" after the children have learned the song). On the words "Every afternoon," he or she taps another child to trade places. Repeat.
Sally [or other child's name] go round the sun.
Sally go round the moon.
Sally go round the chimney pot
Every afternoon.

Johnny Works With One Hammer

Johnny [or any child's name] works with one hammer, one hammer, one hammer
  [pounding motion with one hand],
Johnny works with one hammer, then he works with two.
Johnny works with two hammers, two hammers, two hammers [pounding motion
  with both hands],
Johnny works with two hammers, then he works with three.
Johnny works with three hammers, three hammers, three hammers [add foot to
  pounding motions],
Johnny works with three hammers, then he works with four.
Johnny works with four hammers, four hammers, four hammers [jump up and down,
  still making pounding motions with hands],
Johnny works with four hammers, then he works with five.
Johnny works with five hammers, five hammers, five hammers [add head nodding to
  other motions]
Johnny works with five hammers, then he goes to sleep. [lay head on hands]

Juanito Tiene un Martillo

Juanito tiene un martillo, un martillo, un martillo.
Juanito tiene un martillo, y luego tiene dos.
. . . con dos, tres, cuatro, y cinco, y luego se va a dormir.

SONGS THAT ARE ADAPTABLE TO THEMATIC UNITS

It is often difficult to find enough songs and poems specifically suited to a particular topic. The following songs and chants can be adapted to fit any thematic unit. Just make some simple stick puppets, and you have an instant dramatization.

Five Little Monkeys (Bears, Elephants, Pumpkins)

Five little monkeys jumping on the bed.
One fell off and bumped his head.
Mommy called the doctor
And the doctor said,
"No more monkeys jumping on the bed!" (Repeat, counting down verse by verse to
  one monkey.)

Cinco Monitos

Cinco monitos saltaron alegremente.
Uno se cayó y se pegó en la frente.
Mamá llamó al medicó y dijo fuertemente,
¡Qué paren de brincar inmediatamente!
Entonces . . . cuatro monitos, etc.

One Elephant (Bear, Car, Dinosaur) Went Out to Play
  One elephant went out to play
  On a spider's web one day.
  He had such enormous fun,
  He called for another elephant to come.
  Two elephants went out to play.
  On a spider's web one day.
  They had such enormous fun,
  They called for another elephant to come.
  (Continue with three to ten elephants.)

Un Elefante (Oso, Carro, Dinosaurio) Se Balanceaba
  Un elefante se balanceaba
  Sobre la tela de una araña.
  Como veía que resistía,
  Fué a llamar a otro elefante.
  Dos elefantes se balanceaban
  Sobre la tela de una araña.
  Como veía que resistían,
  Fueron a llamar a otro elefante.
  (Sigue con tres hasta diez.)

Ten Little Brown Bears (Dinosaurs, Ants)
    (sung to the tune of "Ten Little Indians")
  One little, two little, three little brown bears,
  Four little, five little, six little brown bears,
  Seven little, eight little, nine little brown bears,
  Ten little brown bears in a row.

Diez Ositos (Dinosaurios, Hormigas)
  Uno, dos, tres ositos,
  Cuatro, cinco, seis ositos.
  Siete, ocho, nueve ositos.
  Diez ositos chiquitos.

The Wheels on the Bus
  The wheels on the bus go 'round and 'round, 'round and 'round, 'round and 'round.
  The wheels on the bus go 'round and 'round,
  All through the city streets
  The people on the bus go up and down, up and down, up and down.
  The people on the bus go up and down,
  All through the city streets.
  The wipers on the bus go swish, swish, swish, swish, swish, swish, swish, swish, swish.
  The wipers on the bus go swish, swish, swish,
  All through the city streets.
  The baby on the bus goes wah, wah, wah, [and so on].
  The money on the bus goes clink, clink, clink, [and so on].

Las ruedas del bus

Las ruedas del bus van ran, ran, ran, ran, ran, ran, ran, ran, ran.
Las ruedas del bus van ran, ran, ran por toda la ciudad.
La gente del bus sube y baja, sube y baja, sube y baja.
La gente del bus sube y baja por toda la ciudad.
Las monedas del bus hacen clin, clin, clin clin, clin, clin, clin, clin, clin, etc.
La bocina del bus va tu, tu, tu tu, tu, tu tu, tu, tu, etc.
Los bebés del bus hacen bua, bua, bua bua, bua, bua bua, bua, bua, etc.
Sus padres del bus hacen chi, chi, chi chi, chi, chi chi, chi, chi, etc.

Follow-Up Activity

1. This song lends itself to having the children create more verses, with accompanying noises and movements. Brainstorm other things that could happen on a bus and make up new verses.

2. Transfer the verses onto large pieces of construction paper—one verse per page. Have the children pair up, and then have each set of partners illustrate a verse. (You might want to provide the outline of a bus.) Bind all the pages together to make a class book.

3. Tape-record the children singing the song according to the class book. Place the book and the tape in the listening center for repeated listenings at free-choice time.

7

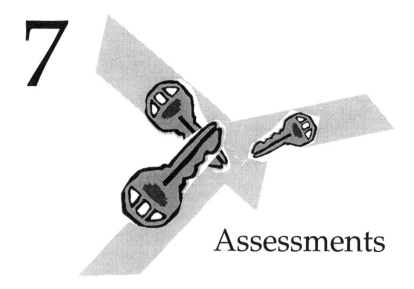

Assessments

Assessment is a daily, ongoing process. The purpose of assessment is to find out both what your students know and how successful your teaching strategies have been. Assess what you plan to teach and what you think you've taught.

CHAPTER CONTENTS

◆

ASSESSMENT OVERVIEW

Authentic assessments are built into the daily activities that students normally do. Any reading, writing, or math assignment provides information about what students know. It is important to collect that information and organize it in some way so that it can inform and guide your instructional decisions.

At the beginning of the year, especially in your first year of teaching, assessment can appear to be an overwhelming and impossible task. Finding the time to sit with an individual student for a period of time is difficult until classroom routines and procedures are established. Therefore, allow time, say 2 weeks, to get your classroom running smoothly before you try any individual assessments. This does not mean you won't be noting what your students know through observation, however.

It is also important to note that it usually takes a couple of weeks for K-1 students to feel comfortable in the school environment. Your assessment information will be more accurate when you have allowed this time for adjustment.

The important types of assessment information you collect on each student should include the following:

- ☑ Samples of student work kept on a regular basis
- ☑ Anecdotal records of your observations of students' involvement in learning activities
- ☑ Individual assessments of the objectives of the curriculum

The following are some considerations about assessment:

- ☑ Attempt to assess only what will be useful to you for planning instruction, reporting to parents, and meeting district requirements.
- ☑ Plan a series of assessments—don't try to assess all the grade-level expectations at once. Expect to assess skills at least once a quarter in addition to the beginning of the year.
- ☑ Be familiar with the report card form, the parent conference form, and so on to be sure you assess what you are expected to report.
- ☑ Try to do the assessments yourself. The process a student goes through in answering a question is often more instructive to you than the answer.
- ☑ In intermediate grades, tell the students what you will be looking for. Eventually, students can participate in the process of establishing assessment criteria.

Getting Started

Assessment Box: K-1

Prepare a box or Ziploc bag with all the materials you will need (e.g., pieces of construction paper of all the colors, shapes, counters, alphabet cards, sequence cards, numbers) to test the objectives you are required to report. Include in the box or bag the individual student record sheets you will be using to record the information. Having all the assessment materials organized in one spot will facilitate your being able to take advantage of spare moments to make assessments.

Anecdotal Records: K-6

Anecdotal records help you to focus on an individual student on a regular basis. You should plan on spending at least part of each day focusing on 5 to 6 children and writing your observations about what they are doing and saying, what they are interested in, and so on. If you observe 5 or 6 students a day, you will be observing each child once a week. Even if you observe only 2 or 3 students a day, you will build up an impressive record over the year.

Observations can occur throughout the day. Think through your daily schedule to find a few minutes here and there that you could devote to observation.

Many times, the task of keeping anecdotal records organized defeats teachers, and they give up on keeping them. Following are several ideas for how to organize the process. Choose one that you think fits your style.

- Make a notebook with dividers for all students. Carry binder paper on your clipboard. Put the child's name and the date at the top of the page. Record your observations. File the binder paper in the notebook at the end of the day. Or eliminate filing at the end of the day by carrying the binder with you and writing in it directly.
- Make a file box for index cards with a divider for each student. Each day, make a file card for each of the children you will be observing that day, including the date. Carry the file cards on a clipboard and make your notes on them. File the cards at the end of the day.
- Purchase peel-off address labels or Post-it Notes, and carry these on your clipboard. Record your observations of each student on a separate label (remember to write the child's name and the date). At the end of the day, peel off the labels and stick them on the inside of the students' file folders.

Making anecdotal records a part of your daily routine will pay off when it comes to parent conference time as well as help you to understand the development of each student in your classroom.

Samples of Student Work

K-1. Plan to keep student work on a regular basis—once a week if possible. Be sure to date the work. Types of student work you might want to keep include self-portraits, writing samples, art projects, easel paintings, photocopies of journal entries, photocopies of pages read to you (with errors marked), and reproductions of math work. File the same entry for each student during any given week (e.g., file a self-portrait for everybody during Week 1, a writing sample during Week 2, a painting in Week 3, a math paper in Week 4, then start again with a self-portrait). That way, you will build up a compilation of similar types of samples that you can use to document growth or pinpoint areas of need.

Grades 2-6. Make 2 class folders for every student in your class (or have students make them the first day): a reading-writing folder and a math folder. These folders should be set up in a box file in alphabetical order. You will use these folders to collect student work to use for assessment purposes and to document students' growth throughout the year. They will be useful for parent conferences, referrals, and report cards. Don't attempt to save every piece of student work. Students may decide at the end of the month their best 2 or 3 pieces, or you may choose a variety of kinds of work to save.

What goes into the student folders? Assignments you have coded SF (for student folder) in advance, any assessments, student or parent questionnaires, any significant pieces of student work that demonstrate growth or need—all these are things you'll want to save.

Assessment is a critical part of your classroom. Unless you know your students' interests and abilities, you cannot meet their needs with an appropriate curriculum. Spending some time getting to know your students through observation, samples of work, and assessment of skills will give you more confidence in how much your students really do grow and change.

ASSESSMENT FORMS

Checklist for Oral Reading

Assessment of oral reading should be done with students reading individually to you, either during silent reading time or in a private conference. If you do any writing as a student reads, it should be as unobtrusive as possible, and you should assure the student you have confidence in him or her and that you are just making notes to help you remember how well he or she reads. Information may be checked off on this form or listed later in an anecdotal record.

Reading material _____ Date _____

Reading Fluency
[ ] Very slowly, sounding out each word
[ ] Word by word
[ ] Quickly in phrases

Decoding Strategies for Unknown Words
[ ] Looks for biggest known chunks (morphemes)
[ ] Sounds out syllable by syllable
[ ] Sounds out letter by letter

Note particular decoding errors, group errors.

Punctuation
[ ] Ignores punctuation
[ ] Stops for periods but shows no expression
[ ] Expression appropriate to punctuation

General
[ ] Reading material held too close or too far away (eye problem?)
[ ] Uncomfortable, didn't like reading
[ ] Doesn't respond appropriately to comprehension checks

How Challenging Is This Book for the Student?
[ ] Very easy
[ ] Enjoyable
[ ] Challenging
[ ] Frustrating

Oral Reading and Comprehension Assessment

Find 3 different consecutive levels of text. Copy a selection from each, or use those provided by your district. Have students read a single copy of each passage; have multiple copies for yourself to use for recording. Have the text header show the student's name and date, and allow space for tracking individual errors and scoring.

First, allow time for student to read the passage silently. When he or she reads the passage aloud, note errors, using the Oral Reading Miscue Code, which follows. Ask the series of Reading Comprehension questions given on the next page. When completed, thank the student, score his or her performance according to the comprehension rubric, given on the page following, and call on the next student. Information gleaned from these assessments will help you determine the instruction needed for both individuals and groups of students. It will also help determine each student's appropriate literature level. This method, when used regularly, ensures that students are guided by accurate information about their developmental needs.

Oral Reading Miscue Code

Student	*Teacher Response*	*Record (example)*
Reads correctly	Listen, follow along	Nothing
Misreads a word	Write the error above the word on copy	sleep slept
Omits a word	Cross out the word	*as
Adds a word	Insert the word with a caret	ever when ^ she arrives
Doesn't know a word, looks to you for assistance	Tell the student the word (no prompting), write "T" above	T apartment
Self-corrects an error	Write "sc" above the word	SC tight
Repeats or rereads a word, phrase, or sentence	Write "r" above the word or, for a phrase or sentence, indicate where she or he began rereading	r repairman _____ r a jukebox repairman
Uses phonics to sound out words	Write "ph" above the word	ph trade

Reading Comprehension Questions

Student: _____   Date: _____
Book Title: _____   Book Level: _____

Ask the student to read and answer the following questions. Let your student know he or she may refer back to the text, if necessary. Use a highlighter to score student responses, or highlight portions within each section.

☑ Retell the story in your own words.

☑ Describe a character in the story. How did that person look and act? How did other characters react to him or her? How do you know?

☑ What would be a good title for the story, and why?

☑ If the story were continued, what might happen next?

☑ What was the most important event in the story? Why?

Reading Comprehension Rubric

Student: _____ Date: _____
Book Title: _____ Book Level: _____

	1	*2*	*3*
A	Retold story out of sequence, with some incorrect information about events and when they occurred	Retold major events of story in correct sequence, with few details	Retold story, in sequence, clearly identifying and describing the beginning, middle and end of story—may have identified a problem and solution
B	Described a character with few details, omitted evidence to support opinions	Described some aspects of the character, omitted evidence to support opinions	Described a character in detail and supported opinions with evidence from the text
C	No ideas for a new title, or title does not fit story	Appropriate title	Creative title with justification
D	No prediction, or the prediction is not a logical extension of story	Reasonable prediction	Reasonable, descriptive prediction that clearly defines in detail what might happen next
E	Identifies an event that may not be a key event, does not support opinion with evidence	Identifies a key event and gives a plausible reason for the selection based on facts in the story	Identifies a key event and clearly describes why it is a key event, connecting literal and inferential information found in text

Other Quick Reading-Writing Assessments

Five-Finger Test

This is a student self-assessment of independent reading level. Teach your students this quick method of determining their independent reading level early in the year:

1. Choose a book.

2. Choose a page and read silently to yourself.

3. Place a finger on each unknown word on one page.

4. When 5 fingers have been placed on a single page, you may decide that the book is too difficult for you to read alone.

5. Choose another book and begin again.

6. List in your reading record the book you decide to read.

Quick Sorts

Quick sorts are short, quick tests, usually for decoding or sight word reading ability. They are useful for a quick snapshot of where individual students are in these areas and will help you in grouping students to work on decoding and sight word skills. They should not be used to determine a child's reading placement for the rest of the year. Some examples of quick sorts are, for English reading, the San Diego Quick Assessment and the Slosson; for Spanish reading, the Santillana Quick Placement.

Assessing Student Writing

During the first month of school you will want to collect samples of several types of writing from students. These might include creative stories (from the Wiggly Line worksheet), letters (their letters to you), factual writing ("Who Lives at My House"), reflective writing (journals), and creating questions (various interview activities). Saving samples of each of these over time will allow you to see whether growth is taking place in both content and form. You won't have the time to record a detailed analysis of all the information that each piece can reveal, so you will need to scan for particular aspects that will inform your immediate instruction and help students focus on goals for themselves.

A simple way to do this is to sort the writing samples into 3 stacks: (a) those papers that show developing or emergent qualities, (b) those papers that show capable writing techniques, and (c) those papers that show strong qualities. See the Writing Rubric and Checklist for Writing Assessment for samples of check sheets that you could use to determine general writing deficiencies within the class so as to instruct your lessons. It can also be used for individual written work to give the students feedback.

Monthly Writing Sample

On the first day of every month, have students write one page of their best writing. You can either have students save these pages in their writing folders or keep the pages posted on a bulletin board, with the current month's work stapled on top.

Checklist for Writing Assessment

This is a checklist for you to use in looking at student work and for notation on the anecdotal record form, not for red-penciling student work. Use this list also to create student proofreading self-assessments. Do not look at every paper for every aspect of writing. Use the information you gather to plan what lessons you will teach. Is it something the whole class will need or just a small group?

Content of Writing, Narrative (any fictional story)

[ ] Is there a sequence—beginning, middle, and end?

[ ] Does a plot develop—problem, response, action, outcome? Is it believable, logical, exciting?

[ ] Are there interesting characters? (Good description?)

[ ] Does the setting add to the story? (Good description?)

Content of Writing, Expository (any nonfiction explanatory writing)

[ ] What kind of organizational structure was used in prewriting? (Matrix, hierarchy, web, outline, list?)

[ ] Are there supporting facts?

[ ] Are there smooth transitions between statements, paragraphs?

Mechanics of Writing

[ ] Was appropriate form used? (Paragraphs, letter format, title?)

[ ] Are there trends in the kinds of grammar errors made?

[ ] What kinds of punctuation or capitalization errors occurred?

[ ] How is the sentence structure? Is there space between words?

Spelling

[ ] Are there phonetic problems, families of words?

[ ] What are the most common misspellings?

[ ] Are misspellings due to oral or aural language problems?

[ ] Is your spelling program covering the errors?

(Spelling programs are a question you'll need to deal with at your school site. If you don't feel the current program is meeting your students' needs, you will need to be able to articulate an alternative to parents and administration clearly before changing your approach.)

Penmanship

[ ] Are there problems with basic letter formation?

[ ] Is motor coordination a problem?

[ ] Is neatness a problem? Is there a difference between a draft and a published copy?

[ ] What could the student do to improve his or her penmanship?

Self-Editing Checklist

_____ I have read my work to myself both silently and aloud.

_____ I have read my work to _____ (classmate/s)

_____ Capitalization: I have checked that every sentence and name starts with a capital letter.

_____ Punctuation: I put periods (.), question marks (?), or exclamation points (!) at the end of each sentence.

_____ Spelling: I underlined words I think are misspelled.

  ☑ I tried different ways to spell them.

  ☑ I used a dictionary.

  ☑ I asked a classmate.

_____ My story has a beginning, middle, and end.

. . . .

Self-Editing Checklist

_____ I have read my work to myself both silently and aloud.

_____ I have read my work to _____ (classmate/s)

_____ Capitalization: I have checked that every sentence and name starts with a capital letter.

_____ Punctuation: I put periods (.), question marks (?), or exclamation points (!) at the end of each sentence.

_____ Spelling: I underlined words I think are misspelled.

  ☑ I tried different ways to spell them.

  ☑ I used a dictionary.

  ☑ I asked a classmate.

_____ My story has a beginning, middle, and end.

Writer's Workshop Observation Guide

When students are working on writing, you will find your class in various stages of the writing process. You will want a simple, efficient way to keep track of what students are working on and where their strengths and needs are. This checklist is designed for assessment of each of the stages of the writing process. As students work, walk around with the Writer's Workshop Class Profile form (or something similar) and make notes on their progress in the particular stages they are working on in the writing process. If you have 30 students, you will need to comment on only 6 each day to cover the entire class by the end of a week. This will leave you plenty of time for individual conferences and other supportive work.

In all stages of the process, it may be useful to note whether students are on task, who they are working with, and what their attitudes seem to be about what they are doing, as well as any areas that you work on with a student. Here are some suggestions to think about at each stage:

Prewriting: Does the student demonstrate organizational skills, brainstorming, mind mapping, outlining, note taking? Does the student have difficulty in this phase? What might the obstacles be?

Drafting: Does the student write fluently? (Note the number of words or lines written.) Does spelling get in the way? Is the student comfortable inventing spelling? (Note topics the student writes on.)

Revision: See the content sections of the Checklist for Writing Assessment for possible areas of revision. What motivates the student to revise? Does the student find his or her own areas of weakness? Whose feedback does the student value?

Editing: See the Mechanics section of the Checklist for Writing Assessment. Does the student become overwhelmed by mechanical problems?

Publishing: What form does the student choose for publishing? (Note how long this process takes and the student's attitude toward publishing the work.)

Remember, the point is not to write copious notes on students but simply to jot down quick observations that will indicate to you where students are and what they were doing on the day that you checked in with them. The Writers Workshop Class Profile shown on the next pages is an example of an observation form.

Writers Workshop Class Profile

Codes for stages: PW = Prewriting, D = Drafting, R = Revising, E = Editing, P = Publishing

Week of _____

Names of Students	Topic or Story	Comments (stage appropriate)

Teaching Students Self-Assessment

Materials: enough teacher-made worksheets for all students, pencils
Grouping: whole class
Approximate Time: 20-30 minutes
Directions:

1. Make your own worksheet or use one of the following examples of a self-assessment.

2. Look over the assessment, go over it with the class. Brainstorm ideas for responses.

3. Pass out the work sheets and explain this activity to the students. For example, you might say something such as,

> The more we know about ourselves, the better choices we can make. This activity will help you reflect on or think about how you feel about things. I will collect and read these work sheets, but the information will remain private. The more thought you put into your answers, the more helpful this activity will be. You will have approximately 15 minutes to complete the work sheet. I will collect the papers when everyone is finished. If you finish early, you may silently read a book.

4. Give the signal to begin, and then circulate around the room, keeping the students on task. You may want to fill out one of the work sheets yourself.

5. When everyone has finished, give the zero-noise signal and collect the papers.

Closure: Ask such questions as, "Did anyone find a question difficult to answer? Which one? Why do you think it was difficult?" (Be prepared to volunteer your own responses. You are modeling for the students that the classroom is a safe place to share ideas and feelings.) Also, be sure to say, "Thank you for your honest responses. They will help me know you better."

Read the worksheets carefully. The responses will give you insight into your students' behavior and how they learn. Some students will be able to analyze their feelings better than others. Keep the worksheets in individual student folders. Do this activity periodically throughout the school year or just once more at the end of the year, and let the students compare their responses.

Student Self-Assessment

Name _____

Write a sentence about each of the following statements.

   1. I like school.

   _____

   2. I'm a responsible person.

   _____

   3. I have many friends.

   _____

   4. I have a close friend.

   _____

   5. I like to read.

   _____

   6. I'm comfortable reading aloud.

   _____

   7. I write stories at home.

   _____

   8. I'm a good writer.

   _____

   9. I'm good at art.

   _____

  10. I'm a leader.

   _____

  11. I'm dependable.

   _____

  12. I like science.

   _____

13. I'm cooperative.

_____

14. I'm good at sports.

_____

15. I'm a fair person.

_____

16. My favorite subject is

_____

17. My least favorite subject is

_____

18. I'm good at

_____

19. I could improve in

_____

20. I read ___ hours a week.

_____

If you would like to add or explain something, please use the back of the paper.

Evaluación Personal del Estudiante

Nombre _____

Escriba un oración por cada uno de los siguientes.

1. A mí me gusta la escuela.

_____

2. Yo soy una persona responsable.

_____

3. Yo tengo muchos amigos.

_____

4. Yo tengo un amigo favorito.

_____

5. A mí me gusta leer.

_____

6. A mí no me molesta leer en voz alta.

_____

7. Yo escribo cuentos en mi casa.

_____

8. Yo soy un buen escritor.

_____

9. A mí me gustan las cosas artísticas.

_____

10. Yo soy un líder.

_____

11. Yo soy cumplidor.

_____

12. A mí me gustan las ciencias.

_____

13. A mí me gusta cooperar.

_____

14. Yo soy un buen deportista.

_____

15. Yo soy una persona justa.

_____

16. Mi materia favorita es

_____

17. La materia que menos me gusta es

_____

18. Yo soy bueno en

_____

19. Yo podría mejorar en

_____

20. Yo leo ___ horas a la semana.

_____

Si quieres explicar o decir algo más, usa el otro lado de la hoja.

How I Feel

Name _____

These sentences are not finished. Complete each sentence by writing what you feel. Remember, there are no right or wrong answers.

1. I'm really interested in

2. What I like best about myself is

3. Sometimes, I worry about

4. I am happy when

5. I get upset when

6. If I could change myself, I would

7. My best experience in school was

8. I need help with

9. I wish that

Como Siento Yo

Nombre _____

Estas oraciones no están completas. Termina cada oración describiendo cómo te sientes. Recuerda, no hay contestaciones correctas o equivocadas.

1. Lo que más me interesa es

2. Lo que más me gusta acerca de mi mismo

3. A veces lo que más me preocupa es

4. Estoy feliz cuando

5. Me da coraje cuando

6. Si pudiera cambiar algo de mi mismo, cambiaría

7. Mi mejor experiencia escolar fue

8. Necesito ayuda con

9. Yo quisiera que

What I Think About Reading

Name _____ Date _____

1. How do I feel about reading?

2. How much time do I read and when do I do it?

3. When I can read anything I choose, I read

4. I like to read books and stories about

5. The best books or stories I have ever read were

6. The things I don't like about reading are

7. What I would like to do in reading this year is

8. The way I will become a better reader is to

Moran, C., Stobbe, J., Baron, W., Miller, J., & Moir, E. Keys to the Classroom, Second Edition. Copyright © 2000, Corwin Press, Inc.

Lo Que Yo Opino de la Lectura

Nombre _____ Fecha _____

1. ¿Cómo me siento acerca de la lectura?

2. ¿Cuánto tiempo me paso leyendo y cuando leo?

3. Cuando puedo leer cualquier cosa, yo escojo

4. Me gusta leer libros y cuentos acerca de

5. Los mejores libros o historias que yo he leído

6. Lo que no me gusta acerca de la lectura es

7. Lo que yo quisiera hacer este año en la clase de lectura es

8. De la manera que voy a ser un mejor lector va a ser

What I Think About Writing

Name _____ Date _____

1. How do I feel about writing?

2. The kinds of writing I enjoy most are

3. The hardest thing about writing is

4. The best things I've ever written were

5. Some of the things I would like to do better in my writing are

6. Some of the things I do well in my stories are

Lo Que Pienso Acerca de la Escritura

Name _____ Date _____

1. ¿Cómo me siento acerca de la escritura?

2. De la siguiente lista, el tópico para escribir que me daría más placer sería

3. Lo más difícil para poder escribir es

4. Las mejores cosas que he escrito son

5. Algunas de las cosas que quisiera hacer mejor cuando escribo son

What I Think About Math

Name _____ Date _____

1. After a math assessment, I feel
_____ nervous about how I did.
_____ confident and proud about how much I knew.
_____ just okay.

2. When new math ideas are introduced, I usually
_____ pick them up right away.
_____ need some extra help.
_____ feel lost.

3. My parents
_____ are good at math and like it.
_____ tell me they never were good at math.
_____ I don't know whether they like math or not.

4. My favorite kind of math is
_____ computation.
_____ problem solving.
_____ neither of these. I really don't like math.

5. I think
_____ boys perform better than girls in math.
_____ girls perform better than boys in math.
_____ there's no difference between boys and girls in math.

6. When I think about my future career, I might
_____ need to use a lot of math.
_____ choose a career that doesn't use math at all.
_____ figure I can learn whatever math I'll need to use.

7. Something that helps me learn math

_____

8. My favorite type of math is _____

Partner Surveys

Materials: prompts
Grouping: whole class, lined up horizontally
Approximate Time: 20 minutes
Introduction: Ask students to silently stand in a horizontal line (on a piece of tape). Tell students they will be moving after each statement, depending on how they feel they agree or disagree with the statement. The *far-left* side of the line will be for those who disagree with the statement; the *far-right* side is for those who agree. Ask what students will need to keep in mind when moving from place to place.

Posing the following statements, have students move as appropriate for *agreement* and *disagreement:*

- At home, I read a lot.
- Math is one of my favorite subjects.
- If I could, I'd practice art all day.
- I really look forward to PE.
- I consider myself a writer-author.
- I am very comfortable using the computer.
- I love to talk.
- I like to build and fix things.
- I like to sing.
- This year, I would love to be in a play.

Have students take their seats, several at a time: Call those born in January and December; progress through the year.

When all the students are seated, put the statements on an overhead projector and ask students to write descriptions of themselves in relation to the statements. Ask them to add other details about their feelings toward school or academic tasks.

8

Parent Communications

Sample Letters in English and Spanish

Positive communications with your students' parents will strengthen your classroom in many ways.

Dear Parents:

It's hard to believe that summer is almost over, but here we are, about to embark on what I hope will be an exciting and productive year for your child. I am anxious to see that we have a smooth beginning. To ensure that, I am listing a few of the ways you can help _____ adjust to his or her first day of school.

1. To alleviate your child's first-day fears, talk to him or her about what to anticipate: that school will be a fun, busy learning time.

2. Arrive early (anytime after_____), to room _____, next _____, so that I can have an opportunity to greet you.

3. Once the first school bell rings, I will ask all parents to leave the room. This will make it easier for the children and me to bond and will facilitate your child's adaptation to school. I do want parents in the classroom later on, because I strongly believe that your involvement is a key to your child's success. I will be making a strong plea for parent volunteers in a few weeks.

4. If your child rides the bus home that first day, assure him or her that you will be waiting at the bus stop when he or she arrives. I will have a list of the bus stops posted in the classroom.

I am looking forward to meeting you!

Dear Parents:

Estimados Padres:

Parece méntira que ya casi se terminó el verano, pero así es y estamos a punto de embarcarnos en un nuevo año escolar. Espero que sea un año productivo y estimulante para su hijo or hija. Mi mayor deseo es que el principio de este año sea tranquilo. Para asegurarnos de que _____ se adapte fácilmente en su primer dia de escuela, les sugierio lo siguiente:

1. Para reducir a la ansiedad del primer di de escuela, platique con el o ella tocante a lo que puedan anticipar: Que ir a la escuela es divertido y que van a estar may ocupados aprendiendo muchas cosas nuevas.

2. Llegue temprano (despues de las _____), al salón _____ el próximo _____, para yo tener la oportunidad de darles la bienvenida.

3. En cuanto suene la campana, yo les voy a pedir a todos los padres que se retiren del salon. Así el vinculo entere los niños y la maestra se establese y es más fácil la adaptacion de los niños a la escuela. Mas adelante SI voy a querer la presencia de los padres en el salón porqué yo creao que le clave del éxito escolar es su participación. En unas semanas voy a pedirles a los padres vigorozamente que sirvan de voluntarios en el salón.

4. Si sus hijos se van en el camión primer día, asegúreles a ellos que Uds. van a estar esperandolos en la parada cuando lleguen. En el salón voy a tener una lista de las paradas del camión.

¡Estoy anticipando el gusto de conocerlos!

Dear Parents:

Donation List

We are in need of some materials for our art center. If you have any of these items to donate, we would greatly appreciate it.

Fabric scraps
Paper towel rolls
Colored pencils
Buttons
Shells
Seeds, beans, peas
Yarn
String
Ribbon
Different shapes of macaroni
Popsicle sticks
Needles and thread
Felt pieces
Small wood scraps
Squares of cardboard
Felt-tip markers (fat and thin)
Toothpicks
Straws
Bottle caps
Spools
Measuring cups and spoons
Sponges (old)
Old shirts

Estimados Padres:

Lista de Donativo

También necesitamos algunos materiales para el centro del arte. Si ustedes tienen algunos de estos materiales disponibles para donarlos, se lo agradeceremos mucho.

Pedazos de tela
Rollos de toallas de papel
Lápices de colores
Botones
Conchas de mar
Semillas, frijoles, chicharos
Estambre
Cordón
Listón
Macarrón de diferentes figuras
Palitos de paletas
Hilos y agujas
Tela de fieltro
Pedazos de madera chicos
Cuadros de cartón
Plumones (gordos y delgados)
Palillos
Popotes
Corcholatas de botella
Carretes de hilo vacíos
Tazas y cucharas para medir
Esponjas (viejas)
Camisas viejas

Dear Parents:

Our class has voted to have a daily snack at approximately _____. It was decided that each child who wanted to participate would bring a "healthy snack" about once a month. I will send home a note announcing your child's day to bring a snack. Some suggestions are crackers, cheese, fruit, baked goods, nuts, raisins, granola, popcorn, carrots, celery, or other vegetables. There are generally _____ people in the classroom.

Your support in this program is appreciated. If you would prefer that your child not participate, just send a note or call. If you have any other questions or concerns, feel free to get in touch.

Thank you,

Your child is scheduled to bring a snack on _____.

Estimados Padres:

Nuestra clase ha votado a favor de tener un bocadillo a las _____ aproximadamente. Se decidió que cada niño o niña que quiera participar traiga "un bocadillo nutritivo" una vez al mes. Voy a mandar un recado indicándoles el día que les va a tocar traerlo a su niño o niña. Algunos de los bocadillos que sugerimos son gallestas, queso, fruta, postres horneados en casa, nueces, pasas, granola, palomitas de maiz, zanahorias, apio, o alguna otra verdura. Por lo general hay ____ personas en la clase.

Su apoyo en éste programa será muy apreciado. Si prefieren que su hijo o hija no participe en éste programa, nada más manden un recado o comuníquese por teléfono conmigo. Si tienen Uds. alguna pregunta o algo les preocupa comuníquese conmigo con confianza.

Gracias,

El día que le toca a su hijo o hija traer bocadillo es _____.

Dear Parents:

I realize you are busy with your jobs, lives, and families. If time permits, I'd love your help in the classroom. Please take a few minutes to look over the following list to see if you can help.

[ ] *Typing. Commitment: twice during the year.*

[ ] *Handle book club orders. Commitment: once a month or every 6-10 weeks.*

[ ] *Working with individuals or a small group with math. Commitment: once a month to several times a week.*

[ ] *Listening to children read aloud, any day except Friday. Commitment: once a month to several times a week.*

[ ] *Leading a literature group (leading a discussion of a novel with a small group of children), any day except Friday, 8:45-9:40. Commitment: once or twice a week for the duration of the book.*

[ ] *Room parent (general support and primarily help with the carnival—the children pretty well organize their own parties).*

[ ] *Talking to the class or small group about your career. Commitment: one time, to be arranged after December.*

[ ] *Driving on field trips (you must have insurance and seat belts).*

[ ] *Cooking with small groups of students.*

[ ] *Reading to the class once a week, Monday-Thursday, 1:00-1:30.*

[ ] *Anything I missed?*

*If you have any questions or need more information before signing your time away, please call
me at _____.*

Thank you,

_____   _____
Parent's name   *Parent's telephone*

Estimados Padres:

Comprendo que están muy ocupados con su trabajo, vidas, y demás responsabilidades en casa. Si tienen el tiempo, me encantaría tener su ayuda en mi salón de clases. Por favor tome unos minutos para revisar la lista que sigue a ver si pueden ayudarme.

[ ] Escribir en máquina. Obligaciónes: solamente dos veces al año.

[ ] Hacerse cargo de tomar las ordenes del Libro del Mes. Obligaciones: una vez al mes o, cada 6-10 semanas.

[ ] Dirigir un grupo de literatura (dirigiendo una discusión de una novela con un grupo de niños), cualquier día excepto viernes, 8:45-9:40. Obligación: una o dos veces a la semana o hasta que se termine el libro.

[ ] Madre o padre de salón (apoyo en general principalmente con el carnaval—los estudiantes más o menos organizan sus fiestas en la clase por sí mismos).

[ ] Visitar el salón y hablar acerca de su ocupación. Obligación: una vez nada más y los arreglos se harán después de diciembre.

[ ] Ayudar a transportar estudiantes en las excursiones de la escuela (se debe tener aseguranza en el carro y cinturones de seguridad).

[ ] Cocinar con un grupo pequeño de estudiantes.

[ ] Leer a la clase en voz alta una vez por semana, lunes-jueves, 1:00-1:30.

[ ] Algo más que se me olvidó mencionar?

Si tienen alguna pregunta o necesitan información adicional antes de comprometer su tiempo, por favor llame al _____.

Gracias,

_____   _____
Nombre de padres   Teléfono de padres

Dear Parents:

This is a note about homework. Your child will have homework every night except Fridays. The intent of the homework is threefold: (a) It helps to build responsibility in the children, as they are responsible for the completion and the transportation of the work; (b) it gives the students an opportunity to practice skills taught in the class; and (c) it gives you a chance to become involved with your child's class work.

Children are most successful with homework if the time and place for work are consistent. A quiet desk to work at and a regular time, such as right before or after dinner, seem to be the most beneficial.

A copy of your student's homework schedule follows. Please keep it as a reminder.

Thank you,

Homework Schedule

Monday:

Tuesday:

Wednesday:

Thursday:

Estimados Padres:

Esta nota es referente a la assignacióareas. Su hijo o hija a tendrá tarea todos los días excepto el viernes. La tarea sirve tres propósitos: (a) ayuda al estudiante a ser responsable hacer el trabajo, completarlo y transportarlo; (b) le dá la oportunidad al estudiante de practicar la habilidad adquirida en la clase; y (3) les dá a Uds. la oportunidad de envolverse con el trabajo escolar de su estudiante.

Los estudiantes tienen más éxito cuando el lugar y el tiempo para hacer la tarea es el mismo. Escoja un lugar determinado y conveniente para que su hijo o hija haga su tarea, guarde sus papeles y recuérdele traerlo a la clase al día siguiente.

En seguida está la lista de los días de tarea. Por favor guárdela como un recordatorio.

Gracias,

Lista de los Dias de Tarea

    Lunes:

    Martes:

    Miercoles:

    Jueves:

Dear Parents:

This year we are working on the writing process. This process involves these main steps:

1. *Prewriting: thinking, getting started*

2. *Rough drafts: writing ideas down*

3. *Revising: making the words clearer, the content more interesting; making additions, deletions, changes*

4. *Editing and proofreading: correcting spelling, grammar, punctuation*

5. *Publishing: completing the finished work, final copy*

Not all writing will go through all 5 steps. Some may go through only Step 2 or 3. In that case, a paper that comes home would be stamped "unedited," which means it was checked for content only.

If your child asks you to read a piece of his or her writing, ask if you are reading it (a) for enjoyment (sharing), (b) for comments about the content (Is it understandable?), or (c) for editing (correcting spelling, punctuation, grammar). Your responses would vary according to the purpose. Here are some suggested comments or questions:

1. *Enjoyment: Wonderful! I really liked this part . . . How did you think of this idea?*

2. *Content: I'm not sure what you mean here. This part is not very clear. Read it out loud to me. It doesn't feel finished—are you going to write more?*

3. *Editing: Is it okay if I write on your paper? Should I use a pen or pencil?*

It is my hope that this will help you and your child enjoy writing and the written word together.

Sincerely,

Estimados Padres:

Estamos trabajando en el proceso de escritura éo. Éste proceso consiste de los siguientes pasos principales:

1.   *Antes de escribir: pensar, prepararce para empezar*

2.   *Escribir: escribir ideas en papel*

3.   *Revisar: hacer las palabras más claras, el contenido mas interesante; agregar, tachar, hacer cambios*

4.   *Repaso y corrección de pruebas: corregir ortografía, gramática, y punctuación*

5.   *Publicación: terminar el trabajo completo, copiar en limpio*

No todos los trabajos de escritura van a seguir los cinco pasos. Algunos trabajos nadamás van a seguir los pasos dos o tres. En ese caso los papeles que los alumnos lleven a casa van tener un sello que dirá "no corregido" lo cual quiere decir que solamente el contenido ha sido revisado, no la ortografía, gramática o punctuación.

Si su niño o niña le pide a ustedes que lean algo que ellos han escrito, pregúntele para qué propósito: (a) por el gusto de compartir, (b) para comentarios sobre el contenido (¿Se entiende?), o (c) para hacer correcciónes de ortógrafia, punctuación, gramática. Sus respuestas tienen que ser diferentes según el propósito de la pregunta. Los siguientes comentarios o preguntas son recomendables.

1.   *Por el gusto de compartir: Magnifico, de verás me gusta ésta parte . . . ¿Cómo se te ocurrió esa idea?*

2.   *Contenido: No estoy muy seguro/a de lo que quires decir aquí. Ésta parte no está muy clara. Lee esa parte en voz alta. Parece que la idea no ésta completa—¿vas a escribir más?*

3.   *Correcciónes: ¿Puedo escribir en tu papel? ¿Debo usar pluma o lápiz?*

Con la esperanza de que la presente ayude a ustedes y a su hijo o hija gozar la escritura y de la palabra escrita.

Sinceramente,

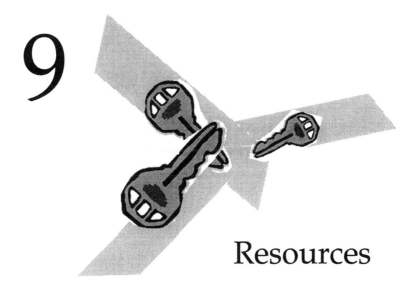

9

Resources

The books in the following bibliography are good sources of activities as are those mentioned in the previous chapters.

CHAPTER CONTENTS

BIBLIOGRAPHY FOR TEACHERS

Conflict Resolution

Kreidler, W. J. (1984). *Creative conflict resolution: More than 200 ideas for keeping peace in the classroom.* Santa Monica, CA: Goodyear.

Literacy

Atwell, N.(1987). *In the middle: Writing, reading, and learning with adolescents.* Portsmouth, NH: Heinemann.

Bear, D., Invernizzi, M. A., & Templeton, S. (1996). *Words their way.* Upper Saddle River, NJ: Prentice-Hall.

Bishop, A. S. (1996). *Teaching phonics, phonemic awareness, and word recognition.* Westminster, CA: Teacher Created Materials.

Calkins, L. M. (1983). *Lessons from a child: On the teaching and learning of writing.* Portsmouth, NH: Heinemann.

Cunningham, P., & Allington, R. (1994). *Classrooms that work: They can all read and write.* New York: HarperCollins.

Cunningham, P., & Hall, D. (1994). *Making words.* Carthage, IL: Good Apple.

Fontas, I., & Pinnell, G. S. (1996). *Guided reading: Good first teaching for all children.* Portsmouth, NH: Heinemann.

Hancock, J., & Hill, S. (1987). *Literature-based reading programs at work.* Portsmouth, NH: Heinemann.

Johnson, T. D., & Louis, D. R. (1987). *Literacy through literature.* Portsmouth, NH: Heinemann.

Johnson, T. D., & Louis, D. R. (n.d.) *Bringing it all together.* Portsmouth, NH: Heinemann.

McCormick-Calkins, L. (1986). *The art of teaching writing.* Portsmouth, NH: Heinemann.

McCraken, R., & McCraken, M. (1978). *Reading, writing and language.* Winnipeg: Peguis.

McCraken, R., & McCraken, M. (1987). *Reading is only the tiger's tail.* Winnipeg: Peguis.

McCraken, R., & McCraken, M. (1987). *Stories, songs and poetry to teach reading and writing.* Winnipeg: Peguis.

Routman, R. (1988). *Transitions from literature to literacy.* Portsmouth, NH: Heinemann.

Routman, R. (n.d.). *Invitations.* Portsmouth, NH: Heinemann.

Tinajero, J., & Schifini, A. (1996). *Into English! Teachers' guide for any level.* Carmel, CA: Hampton Brown.

Math

Baratta-Lorton, M. (1976). *Mathematics their way.* Menlo Park, CA: Addison-Wesley.

Baratta-Lorton, R. (1977). *Mathematics: A way of thinking.* Menlo Park, CA: Addison-Wesley.

Burns, M. (1987). *A collection of math lessons from grades 1 through 3.* New Rochelle, NY: Cuisenaire.

Burns, M. (1987). *A collection of math lessons from grades 3 through 6.* New Rochelle, NY: Cuisenaire.

Burns, M. (n.d.). *The good time math event book.* Concord, CA: Creative Publications.

Cook, M. (1983). *Mathematics problems of the day.* Concord, CA: Creative Publications.

Cossey, R., Stenmark, J. K., & Thompson, V. (1986). *Family math.* Berkeley: Lawrence Hall of Science/University of California Regents.

Day, L., Langhort, C., & Skolnick, J. (n.d.). *How to encourage girls in math and science.* Englewood Cliffs, NJ: Prentice Hall.

Downie, D., Slesnick, T., & Stenmark, J. K. (1981). *Math for girls and other problem solvers.* Berkeley: Lawrence Hall of Science/University of California Regents.

Physical Education

Fluegelman, A. (1976). *The new games book.* Garden City, NY: Dolphin/Doubleday.
Harris, F. (1990). *Games.* Belmont, CA: Fearon Teacher Aids/Simon & Schuster.
Kamiya, A. (1985). *Elementary teacher's handbook of indoor & outdoor games.* Englewood Cliffs, NJ: Prentice Hall.
Larnes, C. (1983). *Awesome elementary school physical education activities.* (Available from the author at 3949 Linus Way, Carmichael, California)

Team Building, Self-Esteem

Gibbs, J. (1978). *Tribes.* Berkeley, CA: Center Source.
Howe, L., Kershenbaum, H., & Simon, S. B. (n.d.). *Values clarification.* Denver, CO: Hart.
Kagan, S. (1988). *Cooperative learning resources for teachers.* San Juan Capistrano, CA: Resources for Teachers.
White, E. (1980). *Nourishing the seeds of self esteem.* Capitola, CA: Whitenwife.

READ-ALOUDS, K-6, IN ENGLISH AND SPANISH

English

Book titles in this list that are followed by asterisks are also available in Spanish.

Kindergarten

Benjamin's 365 Birthdays, Judi Barrett
Caps for Sale, Esphyr Slobodkira
*Corduroy,** Don Freeman
Goodnight Moon, Margaret Brown
Ira Sleeps Over, Bernard Waber
Rosie's Walk, Pat Hutchins
The Snowy Day, Ezra Jack Keats

First Grade

The Carrot Seed, Ruth Krauss
*Curious George,** H. A. Rey
Noisey Nora, Rosemary Wells
Rhymes About Us, Marchette Chute
Stone Soup, Marcia Brown
Tiki, Tiki Tembo, Arlene Mosel

Second Grade

A Birthday for Frances, Russell Hoban
The Carp in the Bathtub, Barbara Cohen
*Frog and Toad Are Friends,** Arnold Lobel
The Island of the Skog, Steven Kellog

Miss Nelson Is Missing, Harry Allard
Stone Soup, Marcia Brown
Sylvester and the Magic Pebble, William Steig

Third Grade

A Bear Called Paddington, Michael Bond
The Borrowers, Mary Norton
*Charlotte's Web,** E. B. White
The Great Brain, Mary Norton
The Lion, the Witch, and the Wardrobe, C. S. Lewis
Miss Rumphius, Barbara Cooney
The Mouse and the Motorcycle, Beverly Cleary
Soup on Fire, Robert Newton Peck
Strega Nona, Tomi DePaola
Stuart Little, E. B. White

Fourth Grade

From the Mixed-Up Files of Mrs. Basil E. Frankweiler, E. L. Koningsburg
The Girl Who Cried Flowers, Jane Yolen
*Island of the Blue Dolphins,** Scott O'Dell
*James and the Giant Peach,** Roald Dahl
Mrs. Frisby and the Rats of NIMH, Robert C. O'Brien
*Ramona the Pest,** Beverly Cleary
*Tales of a Fourth Grade Nothing,** Judy Blume

Fifth Grade

The Incredible Journey, Sheila Burnford
Owls in the Family, Farley Mowat
Philip Hall Likes Me, I Reckon . . . Maybe, Bette Greene
The Pinballs, Betsy Byars
Sign of the Beaver, Elizabeth Speare
Sing Down the Moon, Scott O'Dell
Summer of the Swans, Betsy Byars

Sixth Grade

*Bridge to Terabithia,** Katherine Paterson
Call It Courage, Armstrong Sperry
Ring of Endless Light, Madeleine L'Engle
Roll of Thunder, Hear My Cry, Mildred Taylor
Sounder, Will Armstrong

Spanish

Kindergarten

Corduroy, Don Freeman

Donde Viven Los Monstruos, Maurice Sendak
Historíde la Pollita, Mary DeBall Kwitz
El Oso Más Elegante, Mary Blocksman
El Primer Día Escuela, Helen Oxenbury
Tortillitas Para Mam, Griego y Bucks

Primero

¿Eres tú Mi Mamá?, P. D. Eastman
El Poni, el Oso, y el Manzano, Sigrid Heuck
Jorge, el Curioso, H. A. Rey
Angus y el Gato, Marjorie Flack
Nadarín, Leo Lionni

Segundo

Buenos Días, Querida Ballena, Achim Broger
Osito, Else H. Minarik
Sapo y Sepo, Inseparables, Arnold Lobel
Sylvestre y la Piedra Mágica, William Steig
El Viejo Reloj, Fernando Alonso
Tercero
Aventuras de Connie y Diego, María Garcia
Hansel y Gretel, los Hermanos Grimm
El Patito Feo, Hans Christian Andersen
Ramona la Chinche, Beverly Cleary

Cuarto

La Bruja que Quiso Matar al Sol, Ricardo Alcantara
La Calle es Libre, Kurasa
Platero y Yo, Juan Ramón Jimenez
Telarañas de Charlotte, E. B. White

Quinto

La Isla de los Delfines Azules, Scott Odell
El Mago de Oz, L. Frank Baum
Petrosinella, Basile y Stanley

Sexto

James y el Melocoton Gigante, Roald Dahl
Julie y Los Lobos, Jean Craighead George
El Principito, Antoine de Saint-Exupery
Puente Hasta Terabithia, Katherine Paterson

CORWIN
PRESS

The Corwin Press logo—a raven striding across an open book—represents the happy union of courage and learning. We are a professional-level publisher of books and journals for K-12 educators, and we are committed to creating and providing resources that embody these qualities. Corwin's motto is "Success for All Learners."